Benito Mussolini

Mussolini's Death Scared Hitler

(Insane but True Stories You Won't Believe Actually Happened)

James Hilton

Published By **Regina Loviusher**

James Hilton

All Rights Reserved

Benito Mussolini: Mussolini's Death Scared Hitler (Insane but True Stories You Won't Believe Actually Happened)

ISBN 978-1-7774561-8-4

No part of this guidebook shall be reproduced in any form without permission in writing from the publisher except in the case of brief quotations embodied in critical articles or reviews.

Legal & Disclaimer

The information contained in this book is not designed to replace or take the place of any form of medicine or professional medical advice. The information in this book has been provided for educational & entertainment purposes only.

The information contained in this book has been compiled from sources deemed reliable, and it is accurate to the best of the Author's knowledge; however, the Author cannot guarantee its accuracy and validity and cannot be held liable for any errors or omissions. Changes are periodically made to this book. You must consult your doctor or get professional medical advice before using any of the suggested remedies, techniques, or information in this book.

Upon using the information contained in this book, you agree to hold harmless the Author from and against any damages, costs, and expenses, including any legal fees potentially resulting from the application of any of the information provided by this guide. This disclaimer applies to any damages or injury caused by the use and application, whether directly or indirectly, of any advice or information presented, whether for breach of contract, tort, negligence, personal injury, criminal intent, or under any other cause of action.

You agree to accept all risks of using the information presented inside this book. You need to consult a professional medical practitioner in order to ensure you are both able and healthy enough to participate in this program.

Table Of Contents

Chapter 1: Who Was Mussolini? 1

Chapter 2: Benito's Personal Life 8

Chapter 3: The Start Of Fascism 13

Chapter 4: A Fascist Nation 30

Chapter 5: Throughout World War 2 52

Chapter 6: Mussolini's Early Years 60

Chapter 7: A New Prime Minister 83

Chapter 8: War In Africa 114

Chapter 9: The Path To Another War ... 126

Chapter 10: Italy And Benito Mussolini 154

Chapter 11: What Sort Of Environment Mussolini Lived In? 162

Chapter 12: There Mussolini Was Seeking Help 173

Chapter 1: Who Was Mussolini?

In a way, when we talk about fascism, it is often portrayed as an individual as powerful and brutal like Adolf Hitler, but the term "fascism" was derived from Italian. The concept that came through the bloody Spanish War right before World War 2 and later accepted through Nazi Germany was actually propagated and developed by the Italians at a time in the history of mankind, when huge modifications were implemented, and fear and doubt was all the rage. Mussolini was a powerful and efficient leader. He was an unstoppable person to never be played with. Let's look at his actions and the reasons behind them.

Amilcare, Benito Andrea Mussolini was a Italian journalist and political leader who founded the National Fascist Party and acted as the party's the leader. From the time of March to Rome in 1922 to his removal in 1943 his position as the prime minister of Italy as well as the "Duce" in the era of Italian Fascism from the starting of the Italian Fasces of Battle in 1919, until his assassination by Italian rebels in 1945. In the years between wars, Mussolini, as totalitarian of Italy and a spokesman for fascism, promoted and encouraged the international development of fascist ideologies.

Mussolini was a journalist who began his work as a journalist at the Avanti! newspaper and later as a socialist leader. He joined his National Directorate of the Italian Socialist Party (PSI) in the year 1912 and was sacked for encouraging military action during World War I, which was in opposition to the neutrality policy of the party. Mussolini initiated his Il Popolo d'Italia publication in the year 1914, and fought with the Royal Italian Army till he was wounded and then removed in 1917. Mussolini disapproved of the PSI by focusing his thoughts on Italian nationalists rather than socialism. He then created the fascist party, which opposes egalitarianism and conflict between classes to promote "innovative nationalists" that transcended the boundaries of class. After the March of Rome (28until October the 30th of 1922) The king Victor Emmanuel the Third designated Mussolini as his Prime Minister and made him the youngest person who held the office in that time. Mussolini as well as his followers united the power of a series of laws, which turned the entire country to a one-party government after eliminating the opposition from politics through the secret police and banning strike action by workers. Mussolini achieved his dictatorship by legal and unconstitutional means within five years and was looking for a state that was totalitarian. Mussolini along with the Holy See agreed to sign the Lateran Treaty in the year 1929. This was the year that the Holy See established Vatican City.

With the increase of Italian settler conquers as well as the fascist sphere of influence The goal of Mussolini's diplomatic strategy was to restore the Empire's glory of the past. The 1920s saw him commanded his troops to carry out the Pacification of Libya, ordered the bombardment of Corfu due to a dispute with Greece and established an area of protection over Albania and annexed the city of Fiume to the Italian state via Yugoslavian settlements. In the aftermath of the 2nd Italo Ethiopian War, which took place in 1936 Ethiopia had been destroyed and included in the Italian East Africa (AOI) along with Eritrea as well as Somalia. Albania was invaded by Italian forces during the year 1939. The year 1939 was that time during the Spanish Civil War, Mussolini approved the effective Italian military intervention within Spain to support Francisco Franco between 1936 and 1939. Mussolini's Italy tried to prevent a second world war from starting by deploying troops at Brenner Pass to stop the outbreak of war.

Brenner Pass in order to prevent Anschluss as well as taking part of the Stresa front and the Lytton Report and the Treaty of Lausanne, the Four-Power Pact, and the Munich Agreement. In the end, when it joined Germany along with Japan, Italy separated itself from Britain as well as France. The 1st of September, 1939, Germany attacked Poland, sending war-related statements to France as well as Britain. U.K. and the start of the second world conflict.

Mussolini agreed to be a part of Mussolini's Axis forces on the 10th of June on the 10th of June, 1940. In spite of his initial victory, Mussolini lost the support from the masses and people belonging to his Fascist Party as the Axis was defeated on many fronts as well as the greatest Allied invasion of Sicily. This led to his Grand Council of Fascism passed the motion of no confidence to Mussolini in the early morning of July 25th in 1943. Later that day the king Victor

Emmanuel the Third ousted Mussolini as his Prime Minister. He also placed him under the prison cell, deciding to send Pietro Badoglio for his best friend. Mussolini was released from prison during the Gran Sasso raid by German paratroopers, as well as task forces of the Waffen-SS under the leadership of Significant Otto-Harald Morris on September 12 in 1943, following the King signed an armistice to the Allies. After a meeting with the rescued previous totalitarians, Hitler put Mussolini to be the leader of the Italian Social Republic (Italian: Repubblica Sociale Italiana, RSI) generally referred to as"the" Sal Republic, leading to the civil conflict. Mussolini as well as his wife Clara Petacci tried to get out of Switzerland towards the end of April 1945 following an almost complete defeat. However, both were captured in by Italian communist partisans. They were shot dead by a shooting squad on the 28th of April 1945 close to Lake Como. Mussolini and his partner were later transferred to Milan and their remains were exposed as suspended upside-down at an oil station.

Chapter 2: Benito's Personal Life

Knowing the origins of a person will help us to understand the motives behind their actions. It is important to understand the history of Italian dictator, and discover the source of his ideas.

Mussolini was born in Dovia di Predappio, a tiny town situated in the Romagna region of Forli On the twenty-ninth of July in 1883. Later, in the Fascist time, Predappio and Forl were given the names "Duce's town" as well as "Duce's city" where pilgrims would gather at Predappio as well as Forl in order to visit Mussolini's birthplace.

Alessandro Mussolini, Benito Mussolini's father was a blacksmith, and socialist. Rosa (nee Maltoni) the mother of his, was a true Catholic instructor.

Mussolini was known as Benito following the Benito, the liberal Mexican President Benito Juarez, and Andrea and Amilcare in honor of Italian social democrats Andrea

Costa and Amilcare Cipriani due to his father's politics. The mom was able to get him be baptized when he was born. Benito was the third oldest child born to his caretakers or parents. Arnaldo and Edvige as well as his siblings and sisters, accompanied him.

Mussolini used to hang out when he was youngster, working with his dad in the shop.

His father, who adored the 19th century Italian nationalism and humanist tendencies such as Carlo Pisacane, Giuseppe Mazzini and Giuseppe Garibaldi, formed his initial political philosophies.

His father's political beliefs included anarchists, such as Carlo Cafiero and Mikhail Bakunin and army dictatorships like Garibaldi and nationalist beliefs such as Mazzini. Mussolini delivered a speech in 1902, on the occasion of Garibaldi's passing and praised the republican nationalist.

Mussolini was sent to the Salesian monastery boarding school.

The instructor was frequently confronted by other boarders because due to his violent and grouchy low-key and reserved behavior. The school was severely disciplined for hitting a fellow student by using a pencil during the course of an disagreement. Following his enrollment in a non-religious institution located in Forlimpopoli, Mussolini had high marks, was highly regarded by his teachers and he was principal schoolmaster during his month of July in 1901.

Ida Dalser was Mussolini's first wife, with whom was married in Trento in 1914. Benito Albino Mussolini (1915-1942) The child of the couple was born next year. Mussolini got married to Rachele Guidi (his fiancee since 1910, during the month of December 1915. The details of his previous wedding was kept secret due it was a sign of his political rise and his initial spouse and his child were arrested. Mussolini had three sons, Vittorio (1916to 1997), Bruno (1918-1941) and Romano (1927until 2006) with two daughters: Edda (1910to 1995) and Anna Maria (1929-- 1968) Anna Maria (1929-- 1968), the last of who married Nando Pucci Negri at Ravenna on the 11th of June in 1960. Margherita Sarfatti was a single of Mussolini's female friends along with Clara Petacci, his last lover. According to the biographer of Mussolini, Nicholas Farrell, Mussolini had numerous sexual relationships with his female admirers.

Mussolini's fear of being claustrophobic could have been caused by his the confinement. He was unable to visit heaven Grotto (a cavern in the sea located off the coast of Capri) as well as settling for huge places such as the Palazzo Venezia office, which was 18 by 12 by twelve'm (60 by 40 40 feet).

Mussolini could speak English, French, and an unsteady German along with his own native Italian (his self-confidence led him to not use an German translator). This was important in the Munich Conference, where no any other leader of a nation was able to speak a language other than their own. Mussolini was described as the chief interpreter for the conference "primary translator."

Chapter 3: The Start Of Fascism

Fascism was more prevalent in its peak during the First as well as the Second World War. In this section we'll look at the connection between ideology and conflicts.

Mussolini was transformed following his expulsion from his own party, the Italian Socialist Party because of his support for Italian intervention. He renounced his support of class warfare and embracing revolutionary nationalism that strayed classes. In October 1914, he established the interventionist diary Il Popolo d'Italia and the Fascio Rivoluzionario d'Azione Internazionalista (" Revolutionary Fasces for International Action"), and also the Fascio Rivoluzionario d'Azione Internazionalista (" Revolutionary Fasces for International Action"). In recognition of his support from the nationalists to intervene, he was able the capacity to obtain funding through Ansaldo (an arms firm) as well as other sources for the creation of Il Popolo d'Italia, which was used to motivate revolutionary and socialists to join the military. Beginning in May of the year 1915 French source of information provided additional assistance for Mussolini's Fascists during the time of battle. French social democrats are believed to have been an important source of money, handing aid to social democrats who favored Italian support for France's involvement in the war.

Mussolini attacked socialism orthodoxy on the 5th of December, 1914. He was accused of being unable to grasp that the war was raising the level of nationalism and recognition above the distinction of class.

He completely exhibited his change when he made a statement in which He acknowledged that the nation was an entirely different entity. This was something previously dismissed by him in a speech that stated:

The country hasn't disappeared. The idea that we had was this idea was completely useless. We now see our nation becoming a pulse of real-world reality right in front of our own eyes! ... It is impossible to ruin the country due to the class system. It is a story of customs, mindsets and traditions, languages, cultures, and races, whereas class is the sum of all things to do. It is possible for class to become an important element in the country, however it cannot eliminate the other. In any case where a group of people has not accepted its own rightful ethnic and racial bordersin cases where the nation issue hasn't been resolved - then the struggle for class is an ineffective formula without any effect or effect. Under these circumstances there is a danger that the progress of the class struggle will be hindered by a negative historical background.

Mussolini maintained his campaign the idea of an elite group of advanced leaders in order to rule the society. He advocated for a leadership that was led by innovative and active individuals from every social class and not an elite leadership. Even though he was adamant of socialism as a system, and the concept of the concept of class war, he claimed that he was a nationalist socialist and advocate for the tradition of Italian social democrats of the nationalist tradition such as Giuseppe Garibaldi, Giuseppe Mazzini as well as Carlo Pisacane at the time. The Italian socialist claimed that his inability to be a part of the Italian Socialist Party to renew and change it in line with contemporary realities showed the denial of socialism that was orthodox as being obsolete and ineffective. Mussolini was not alone in his criticism of conventional socialism's failings due to the outbreak in World War I; other interventionist Italian socialists, such as Filippo Corridoni as well as Sergio Panunzio had also slammed the traditional Marxism for its support of the intervention.

Mussolini's political group that was just emerging known as the Fasci d'Azione Rivoluzionaria during 1914, which were known as Fascisti was founded upon these crucial political ideal ideas and visions (Fascists).

The Fascists did not have an integrated set of policies in time time in the 1960s, so they were useless in organizing mass gatherings which was often hounded by officials of the federal government as well as traditional socialists. The conflict between interventionists, such as the Fascists, as well as the orthodox socialists that were anti-interventionist culminated in conflict between both groups. Socialists who were anti-interventionist advanced had their protests and attacks on the Fascists as well as other interventionists became so violent that democratic socialists opposed to the conflict, such as Anna Kuliscioff said that they believed that the Italian Socialist Party had gone too far to suppress the sway of speech that was possessed by those who supported war. The first clashes between Fascists as well as radical socialists shaped Mussolini's perception of the nature of Fascism as a partisan of violence in politics.

Cesare Battisti An irredentist political figure and journalist who was also one of the biggest fans of Mussolini.

Mussolini along with a large number of Italian patriots, decided to fight during the war when WW1 started to take place. Because of his extremist Socialism and his extreme Socialism, he was turned down and was forced to wait for his reserve call. The 31st of August He was taken to the station and was sent back to his former regiment, called the Bersaglieri. He was sent for the Isonzo front after two weeks of refresher training course. He also participated in the Second Battle of Isonzo during the month of September 1915. Then, in October 1915 the program was also involved during the Third Battle of the Isonzo.

The Inspector General then went on to state,

" To ensure quality during military operations," he rose to the grade of corporal. The promotion was deemed to be significant by his outstanding performance and fight skills along with his peace of mind and a lack of worry about suffering, as well as his enthusiasm and dedication to the projects, in which the first priority was any job requiring labor, persistence, as well as his love for and commitment to his tasks.

Mussolini was wounded in battle during February 1917. His injuries were so severe that he was removed from the battlefield.

In his book Diario di guerra, Mussolini describes his experiences in the army. He was for nearly nine months in the frontline of trench combat. He was plagued by paratyphoid during the time. The military career was over in 1917, after he was injured through a bomb in a mortar which exploded inside the dugout. It was discovered that he had around 40 pieces of metal inside the body. He was released from the health center in August 1917. was discharged from the health centre and was able to return to work as editor-in chief for Il Popolo d'Italia. The author released work in which it praised his fellow members of the Czechoslovak Legions within Italy.

In 1915, on the twenty-fifth day of December In Treviglio He married Rachele Guidi as a fellow countrywoman. She had brought to his child Edda and was born in Forli around 1910. He had a son with Ida Dalser, a woman who was from Sopramonte close to Trento and Trento, in 1915. The 11th January of 1916, he officially admitted the child.

The National Fascist Party's Creation

Mussolini the socialist vanished when time the time he came back after The First World War service as part of The Allied forces. It is certain that he was certain that socialism had not worked as a strategy. Mussolini was first elected to the political scene in 1917. He had the help of an L 100 weekly salary of MI5, the British security services MI5 that he employed to ensure that anti-war protestors remained at home and distribute the pro-war propaganda. Sir Samuel Hoare gave his consent to this assistance. Mussolini demanded to see the development of someone that was "callous and able to sweep the country clean" to revitalize the Italian nation in the early years of 1918. Mussolini therefore stated that "socialism as a concept had gone out of fashion; however, it remained in existence only in the form of a protest" until 1919. Mussolini altered the Milan fascio into it was the Fasci Italiani di Combattimento (Italian Battle Team) on the 23rd of March, 1919. The team consisted of 200 people.

Fascism's ideology was formed from many different places. In order to further fascism,

Mussolini used the writings of Plato, Georges Sorel, Nietzsche as well as Vilfredo Pareto's concepts of finance. The work of Plato The Republic was a favorite of his, and he often read it as a source of reasons of motivation. The Republic elaborated upon the ideas of fascism, which is a rule of an elite which advocates the state as the ultimate goal, rejection of democratic principles, the defense of class and cooperation, disapproval of equality, and promoting militarization of the country through the creation of a group of warriors, and requiring residents to take on civic responsibility for the good of the state and applying state intervention in education in order to encourage the development of the war. Plato was a romantic that believed in ethics and fairness, however Mussolini as well as fascism are realists that were driven by political motives.

The diplomacy of Mussolini was founded on the concept of spazio vitale (crucial space) that resembled Lebensraum during German National Socialism.

The idea of spazio vitale first came to light during the year 1919 in which the entire Mediterranean including the so-called Julian March, was redefined to look as an entire area which was part of Italy in the past Roman Province of Italia and was referred to as Italy's specialized sphere of influence. The rights to settle around Slovene ethnic zones as well as the Mediterranean that were likely comprised of tribes that were less industrialized and tribes, was deemed valid by the fact that Italy was probably in a state of overpopulation.

Mussolini stated that the main concern was the fact that "plutocratic" nations such as Britain prevented Italy from achieving the necessary spazio vitale needed to allow the Italian economic growth and expand. The idea was originally conceived by Enrico Corradini in 1914. the natural conflict between "plutocratic" nations like Britain as well as "proletarian" nations like Italy.

Mussolini believed that a country's financial development potential to its geographical location and was of the opinion that the only method to overcome Italy's plight was to acquire the required spazio vitale.

In spite of the fact that the natural tendency to bigoty was more prevalent during Fascism as opposed to National Socialism, the spazio vitale notion had a strong racist undertone from the beginning. Mussolini claimed that it was the "natural norm" which stated that "remarkable" tribal groups, including those of the "barbaric" Slavic tribes of Yugoslavia were to be subjugated to control by "lower" groups. In his speech during the September month in, 1920, he stated: "When confronting a race with as little and as abrasive as the Slavic is, it's best to pursue the stick approach rather than using the one that involves carrots ... The Slavic people should not worry about new victimization ... It is my opinion that the Brenner Pass Monte Nevoso, and the Dinaric Alps must all be an integral part of the Italian frontier ... It is possible to easily trade 500,000 barbarian Slavs in exchange for 500.000 Italians according to my opinion ...

Benito Mussolini, September the 20th of 1920. Pula speech

In the years 1918-1920, during which Italy was part of the Austro-Hungarian regions that included 5100 "Slav" society (for example, Sokol) and a slightly smaller amount of libraries (" reading spaces") were cut off specifically by the Law on Associations (in 1925) and The Law on Public Presentations (in 1926) as well as the Law on Public Order (in 1926)-- which led to the closing of the lyceum that was classical in Pazin as well as that of the Voloska secondary school (in 1918) and the 5 hundred

Slovene and Croatian firstaries. Numerous "Slav" trainers were exiled to Sardinia as well as Southern Italy under pressure.

Also, Mussolini specified that it was legal to Italy to enforce an imperialist agenda in Africa in the sole reason that he thought that all Africans were "inferior" to white people.

Mussolini declared that the entire universe was divided in the hierarchy of race (stirpe) which meant that the entire history of humanity was just the Darwinian battle for power and territory between the various "racial masses." Birth rates that were high in Africa as well as Asia were viewed by Mussolini as well as Eugenics movement within the United States, the UK as well as others European as well as European colonial countries at the time including Brazil (cf. Yellow Danger propaganda), as being a threat for the "white race" and frequently he asked the"so what? "Are the whites and the blacks in the front door?"

Then he would reply "Yeah that's true!" Mussolini was convinced his belief that the U.S.A. was doomed due to the fact that people of color were in the U.S. had a higher birth rate than whites which meant that it was inevitable that blacks would gain control over the country and bring the country down to their levels. It was also believed that Italy had a high population was seen as proof of Italians their spiritual and cultural power, and thus justified in settling areas of the country that, in the opinion of Mussolini were derived from Italy in any case, simply because Italy was the successor country to the Roman Empire. Demography was a matter of fate in Mussolini's mind. Those that had populations growing were destined to be dominant, whereas one with smaller populations were weaker powers that ought to be dying. Therefore, natalism was extremely significant for Mussolini since only through increasing the rate of birth would Italy be able to secure its position as a nation that was capable of winning spazio vitale. Mussolini was convinced that his Italian population should reach sixty million for Italy to win a major conflict, and that's the reason the dictator required Italian women to have more children in order to achieve the goal.

Mussolini as well as the fascists had the capability of being both conventional and advanced in the same time as it is because this was a rarity within the political landscape during the time It is often referred to in the context of "The Third Way" by a few authors.

The Fascisti who were headed by Dino Grandi, one of Mussolini's most trusted confidants, formed armies of veterans from war called"blackshirts" (or squadristi) for the purpose of maintaining order in the roads of Italy. In demonstrations and parades where the blackshirts were confronted by the socialists, communists, and anarchists. these groups were simultaneously fighting one another. Because of the imminent danger and the widespread anxiety about a revolution by communists however, it was the Italian federal government was not able to step into the blackshirts' actions. The Fascisti increased rapidly and at a conference held in Rome two years later, they declared themselves to be as the National Fascist Party. First time, Mussolini was chosen for the Chamber of Deputies in the year 1921. Between the years, Mussolini had some love with Jewish writer and expert Margherita Sarfatti who was dubbed"the "Jewish Mother of Fascism" during the time in the period from about 1911 until around 1938.

Chapter 4: A Fascist Nation

In the wake of all the prelude periods as well as the battles that raged all over the world and the country was in the words of Mussolini prepared for a complete immersion into fascism. We'll discuss it in this section.

Mussolini was the one responsible for a broader set of political changes that created fascism an influential factor within Europe as per German-American historian Konrad Jarausch. He first demonstrated that his party could gain the power of governing a complete federal government in a huge nation that was ruled by fascists and not just appeal to for a future renewal of the country. The movement also stated that it would promote the entire nation and not only a specific segment that was a part of the working classes or the nobles. The movement made an effort to link with those who are often marginalized in the Catholic group. Instead of encouraging businesses to function in the shadows and letting them play the role of a visible actor, he created distinct expectations for them. Then, he established an all-male management cult which brought attention to him and led to a country-wide dispute. Mussolini as a journalist in the past had demonstrated his proficiency in various forms of mass media. This included however, not only more modern media like motion movies and radio. 4th, he conceived the mass-subscription party that had gratis programs for teenagers as well as women and various categories that were easily operated and controlled. The other alternative political businesses as well as parties were shut to him (but this wasn't an actual development at all). In order to scare his opponents by threatening them with the possibility of extrajudicial violence as well as brutality by his Blackshirts, just as they did for all totalitarians.

Mussolini was slowly removing almost all conventional and constitutional limitations on his power from 1925 and 1927. He then created an armed police state. His official title has been changed to "President of the Council of Ministers" to "Head of the Federal government" through a law that was enacted on the night of Christmas, 25th December 1925, within the predominantly Roman Catholic nation, though Mussolini was still referred to as "Prime Minister" in a variety of non-Italian media sources. There was no need to find a solution for Parliament and was only able to be removed at the hands of King. Although the Italian constitution stipulated that ministers are only accountable to the monarch and not to Parliament, it was becoming impossible to control the government in opposition to the Parliament's explicit desire. It was the Christmas Eve law put an end to this policy and established Mussolini as the sole authority on the agenda of the institution. The program of Mussolini ended up becoming legally ruled due to the law. Regional autonomy was taken care of, and the councils and mayors were replaced through podestas voted from Mussolini's Italian Senate.

Mussolini was executed in the very first time on April 7 1926, in the presence of Violet Gibson, an Irish woman, and child of Lord Ashbourne and Lord Ashbourne, who was exiled upon her arrest.

Anteo Zamboni was only fifteen years old, tried to murder Mussolini in Bologna on the 30th of October in 1926. Zamboni was killed right away as well as later. Mussolini had to endure a screwed executed murder attempt at Rome that was carried out by anarchist Gino Lucietti as well as a planned murder plot from Italian Anarchist Michele Schirru , both of which resulted in Schirrru's incarceration and the execution.

In the wake of Zamboni's attempted murder during 1926, other political party affiliations were banned regardless of being aware that Italy was a one-party country since. (with or without his January speech in the Chamber or the adoption of the Christmas Eve law, depending on the origin). The parliamentary elections were canceled within the same year through an electoral law. The Grand Council of Fascism chose only one candidate to be approved by the plebiscite. It was the Grand Council was established 5 years earlier as a political corporation and was later "constitutionalized" and made the highest level of constitutional power in the state. It was the Grand Council, on paper could suggest the demise of Mussolini and, as such, was the only authority to examine authority. It was only Mussolini was able to form his Grand Council and set its schedule. To control the southern part of Italy, and specifically Sicily the Italian dictator chose Cesare Mori as the Prefect for Palermo and set out with the aim to destroy the Mafia any cost. Mussolini stated to Mori on the television cable, "Your Excellency has carte free reign; State power should definitely, absolutely be restored on Sicily." If the laws you have in place hinder your but you don't have to be concerned about it. problem since new legislation are being developed.

Mori was not shy about taking over towns, verbally abusing people, as well as holding children and women for a while for them to surrender up. The name was given to him "Iron Prefect" because of his reckless methods. The examinations of Mori's revealed evidence of the Mafia-Fascist conspiracies during the year 1927 and he was dismissed due to his long-term service during the year 1929 at the time the number of deaths at Palermo Province had dropped from 200 to only 23. Mori was appointed senator by Mussolini in 1927, and fascist propaganda claimed that the Mafia was defeated.

The day of the twenty-fourth March 1929, elections for general elections were conducted in the form the referendum. In at this time the country had been reformed into a single-party state including being ruled by the National Fascist Party (PNF) being the sole legally recognised political party. The political list that was presented was accepted by 98.43 percentage of people.

The "Libyan Pacification"

In 1919 in 1919, the Italian government implemented a number of liberal changes in Libya which included the introduction of Arabic as well as Berber education, as well as the possibility of Libyans becoming Italian citizens.

Mussolini kept the rule of Giuseppe Volpi, who had been chosen in 1921. He rescinded the actions that granted Libyans the right to equality.

The policy of stealing land from people of Libya to transfer to Italian settlements ignited Libyan opposition that was led by Omar Mukhtar, and the Fascist plan was an genocidal plan to murder the most Libyans possible during the ongoing "Pacification of Libya."

In 1931, around 50% of the Cyrenaica population was confined to the 15 prisoner of war camps, and it was the Royal Italian Flying force performed chemical warfare on the Bedouin.

Marshal Pietro Badoglio wrote to General Rodolfo Graziani on the 20th of June 30th, 1930. In it, he wrote "In regard to the general approach, it's necessary to make a clearly defined distinction between the government-controlled people and the insurgent systems." It is my intention to not reduce the significance and importance of this decision and could be the final end for the marginalized people ... However, the path has been mapped out to be followed and we must take it up to the top regardless of whether it will mean dying for the whole population of Cyrenaica.

The 3rd of January 1933 Mussolini spoke to the ambassador Baron Aloisi that French in Tunisia were guilty of an "dreadful error" through allowing sexual relations between French and Tunisians and he believed it could result in the French becoming a country with "half-castes," and to prevent the same scenario occurring to Italians and the Italians, he directed Marshal Badoglio to declare hybrids a crime in Libya.

His Financial Technique

To combat financial collapse and the high rate of unemployment, Mussolini started some public development plans and federal government initiatives throughout Italy. In the Battle for Wheat was his first (and most well-known) initiative, where the creation of 5,000 farms as well as 5 new townships for farmers (consisting in Littoria as well as Sabaudia) were built in the area of land reclaimed from draining in the Pontine Marshes. Mussolinia was a model farming town located in Sardinia was erected, however it was later rebranded Arborea. The hamlet was one of a series of 10s in the dozens of farms which Mussolini would like to create across the country. In the course of this battle, Battle for Wheat drew essential sources from commercially viable agricultural crops and turned them into wheat production. Even though it was true that the landowners utilized all the latest technology to cultivate wheat in the wrong soil the rates soared, consumption declined, and high taxation was imposed regardless of the fact that wheat yield was increasing. Tariffs led to a lot of inefficiency and the farm subsidies offered by the federal government led the country deeper into indebtedness.

Mussolini established the "Battle for Land,"" an approach to land reclamation that was developed in 1928. Although programs like the depletion of the Pontine Marsh for farming in 1935 served as propagandists, provided work to people who had no job, and helped the landowners to control aids, different parts that were part of Battle for Land came a yield. It was the Pontine Marsh was ruined at the time of the Second World conflict due to this policy and was in contradiction to the Battle for Wheat (little plots of land were not properly allocated to support the massive growth of wheat). The poverty of peasants remained high, at under ten thousand people were transferred to the land redistributed. The year 1940 saw in 1940, the Battle for Land project was abandoned.

" The debate cannot be resolved except through State intervention and within the framework of the State," he mentioned in "The Dogma of Fascism" during the year 1930.

The politician attempted to alleviate the recession through the launch of the "Gold to the Fatherland" initiative, that enticed people to donate the gold-colored fashion jewelry of Federal government officials as a reward for steel wristbands with the"Gold for the Fatherland" slogan "Gold to the Fatherland." Rachele Mussolini also gave her wedding anniversary ring to this charity. The gold was collected and then melted into gold bars that was then handed over to nation banks.

The policy of Mussolini included authority over businesses by the government. He stated in 1935 it was the government that ruled three quarters of Italian businesses. The following the same year Mussolini issued a number of decrets aimed at increasing the control of financial assets that included, but not restricted to one that demanded banks, corporations and individuals to transfer all foreign-issued bonds and stock possessions into the Bank of Italy. The cost control system was established during the year 1936. Also, he tried to change Italy into an autocratic self-dependent state by imposition of trade restrictions that were high for most countries, excluding Germany.

Mussolini introduced the socialization of finances theory in 1943.

Trains (Trains).

Mussolini wanted to be credited for massive public works initiatives in Italy particularly trains.

"Say whatever you like about Mussolini and his efforts to make the trains work on time" was the most common expression following the improvement he claimed to have made to the network of trains. In 1924, journalist and writer Kenneth Roberts wrote:

The differences between Italian train service during 1919, 1920 and 1921, and the service that was offered during the first year of Mussolini's his power was awe-inspiring. Trains ran on time The cars were neat personnel were efficient as well as enjoyable. The trains arrived and left promptly on timeand not 15 minutes. in the dark, and not 5 min. not 5 min. late, but just in the moment.

Actually, prior to the time Mussolini was elected in Italy, the country's terrible postwar train system was beginning to expand.

The development was more apparent than actual. In 1954, Bergen Evans wrote:

The writer was a driver with the Franco-Belgique Tours Company in the period of summertime in 1930. This was that time of Mussolini's peak time in which every train was protected with a fascist. He is adamant that all Italian trains in which he traveled weren't at timeor close to they were. There must be thousands of people that can support the claim. The issue is minor however it is something that should be kept on your mind.

While the trains that carried visitors to shows usually, though sometimes not always in time but the same did not apply to lower lines, in which hold-ups were common in the words of George Seldes in the year 1936. Ruth Ben-Ghiat has mentioned that "they improved the lines and were of political significance in the lines that had political significance to."

His Personality's Propaganda and Cult

His main objective was to make use of propaganda in order to control the Italian population's mind. The routine was aimed at promoting a rich fan cult that focused on his image. The actor posed as the latest fascist Ubermensch by promoting an unrestrained Machismo style, which attributed his abilities as quasi-divine. Mussolini was in charge of the ministers of internal affairs, foreign affairs and people, as well as firms as well as defense work at various times following 1922. He was in charge of up to seven departments at one time and also the presidency. He also served as the head of the powerful Fascist Party and the MVSN which was also known as "Blackshirts," an armed regional fascist militia, which terrorized the beginning of resistance within cities and provincial areas. In the future, he was to create the OVRA and OVRA, a clandestine group of police force that had the backing of the main state. As a result it was possible for him to keep the power he held and prevent any rivals from coming into the picture.

Mussolini was also portrayed as a talented athlete and artist. The teachers in the universities and schools were required to swear an oath of support for the Nazi programme. Mussolini selected all newspaper editors. Only who had a valid certification by the Fascist Party were permitted to be journalists. Mussolini skilledly created the notion of the concept of a "free press" through the release of these certificates without revealing the details. Trade unions also were stripped of their freedom and were forced to be part of what was known as "corporative" or "corporative" structure. The goal, which was guided by guilds of the middle age and never fully realized, was to include the entire population of Italians in a variety of professional associations or companies and all of them could be subject to veiled the federal government's control.

The bulk of the money was used to fund notable public works as well as a famous worldwide businesses. Heaven Riband Ocean ship SS Rex, the world's fastest seaplane Macchi M.C. 72, as well as Italo Balbo's transatlantic flight boat journey, which was greeted by a roaring crowd throughout America U.S. when it landed in Chicago during the year 1933. They were also among them.

The forms of the Fascist idea were outlined by a 1932 article within the Enciclopedia Italiana by popular theorist Giovanni Gentile and Mussolini himself. A few historians are in agreement on the representations of

Mussolini as a scholar. Gunther described his character as "most likely to be among the smartest and smartest of autocrats" and was the sole intellectual national leader of the 1940s. "His ability to comprehend modern philosophical and political writing was, at a minimum, as good than any contemporary European political leader," German historiographer Ernst Nolte noted.

After World War I, nationalists believed that they were fighting powerful and liberal institutions created by federal governments such as Giovanni Giolitti's. This is why they embraced traditional education. According to Filippo Marinetti in 1919 Futurism is an original culture movement which would serve as the driving force behind Fascism and was marketed as "a institution that emphasized physical strength and patriotic spirit." Marinetti disliked "the today outdated as well as troglodyte Ancient Greek and Latin courses," proposing that they were to be transformed through exercises inspired by Arditi troops (" being taught to carry down knees and hands in facing gilding guns; waiting at a crossbeam that is open that is able to go sideways above their heads, etc"). The very first Fascist young wings Avanguardia Giovanile Fascista (Fascist Youth Vanguards) in 1919, and Gruppi Universalitari Fascisti (Fascist university groups) from 1922, were formed during the time in the year 1922.

After Mussolini's victory in the march on Rome The Fascists began looking at ways to politicize Italian society which included education as a key element. Renato Ricci, a previous director of arditos and deputy secretary of the Ministry of Education, was assigned with Mussolini with "rearranging youth's lives both from a physical and moral perspective." Ricci was in contact on the subject with Robert Baden-Powell, the creator of Scouting and Scouting in England as well as Bauhaus artists from Germany in search of the motivation. Mussolini's orders of April 3rd, 1926 was the basis for an opera called the Opera Nazionale Balilla, which was helmed by Ricci over the following 11 years. Aged between 8 and 18 years old, the children were divided into two groups, namely The Balilla as well as the Avanguardisti.

" Fascist schools are moral and physical as well as social as well as military-related," Mussolini said, "and attempts to create an entire, harmoniously shaped human being, one that is a fascist as per our ideals." Mussolini designed this system by keeping the psychological aspect of development with this in mind: "Performances, theories, as well as abstract concepts aren't enough for feeding the teenage and youth the years of. What we are trying to convey should at first inspire their imagination, later into their hearts and finally, to their intelligence ".

The old methods were meant changing through "academic values developed by actions and examples." Fascism was a battle against rationalism through the variation in idealism as well as the Opera Nazionale Balilla was used to evade academic norms through imposing the shared structure, as well as Mussolini's personal persona the cult.

Roman Catholicism was another substantial element of Fascist culture policy. An agreement with the Vatican was signed in the year 1929. It put an end to the decades-long disagreement with both the Italian government and Papacy beginning in the aftermath of your Savoy's taking over the Papal States throughout the marriage of Italy in 1870. It was the Lateran Treaties, which finally recognized the sovereignty of the Italian state's independence through it's Roman Catholic Church and acknowledged the autonomy from Vatican City by the Italian state, were well accepted by the church hierarchy they Pope Pius XI called

Mussolini "the man to be praised by Providence."

The 1929 agreement contains an agreement that legally requires to the Italian Federal government bring charges against those who violate the law to ensure that respect for the honor of the Pope as well as self-respect.

Mussolini was baptized again as the Roman Catholic priest in the year 1927. In his anti-communist opinions, Mussolini helped numerous Catholics to support him in the years following 1929.

Chapter 5: Throughout World War 2

Mussolini played a significant role during World War 2, and his influence, alliances and opposition to Hitler's orders are not to be overlooked. We'll look at the things he accomplished during this critical time in the history of.

The obsession of Mussolini with demography in the 1930s' end made him believe that Britain as well as France were in fact two powers as well as that Germany as well as Italy were, for no other reason but their math power was destined to dominate Europe. Mussolini declared that France's declining birth rate was "exceptionally horrendous" and claimed that his British Empire was doomed because quarter of the populace was older than 50. This was the reason why Mussolini was of the opinion that an alliance with Germany would be more appropriate than aligning with Britain as well as France as it would be better suited to be allies to the strong, not those who were less powerful. International politics, as per Mussolini as he saw it, was an issue of Social Darwinian dispute between "virile" states that had large birth rates as well as "effete" states with low birth rates. Mussolini believed that France as an "weak and outdated" nation, claiming that the French mortality rate per week was more than 2,000 times the rate of birth, and he did not want to join forces with the French.

Mussolini was convinced that due to the high rate of births in Italy that it was his destiny to lead his country's Mediterranean that he omitted much of the important plan and preparations required to be able to resolve a conflict with Western nations.

The only reason Mussolini had to not fully aligning with Berlin were his knowledge of Italy's army and financial inexperience, which demanded additional time to prepare, as well as his determination to take advantage of the March 1938 Easter

Accords to divide Britain as well as France. The alliance of the Army with Germany in place of a less shakier and more tolerant association to The Reich in the Anti-Comintern Pact (which had no military commitments) could stifle any possibility that having the Easter Accords being carried out. The Mussolini's Easter Accords, on the side, however, were designed in order to allow Italy to take on its own against France by enhancing relations between the two countries until the point that London will likely to remain neutral in the event the possibility of a Franco-Italian conflict (Mussolini was a royalist who wanted to conquer Tunisia and also was supported by a small portion of the country. It was the Easter Accords, on the contrary, focused upon separating Italy away from Germany.

In a note on Mussolini's notepad dated November 8th of 1938, the count Galeazzo Ciano who was Mussolini's son-in law and the foreign minister laid out his totalitarian diplomacy to France: "Tunisia, with an almost identical system Corsica, Italian and never ever Frenchified which means that it is directly under our control. and the frontier at the river Var," Djibouti would require control as a part of France. Mussolini declared that he didn't have any desire to be involved in Savoy because it was not "traditionally as well physically Italian." On the 30th of November, 1938 Mussolini was pleased to welcome French Ambassador Andre Francois-Poncet to participate in the inaugural ceremony of the Italian Chamber of Deputies, in the time that the crowd of members began to protest their displeasure with France and yelled "Tunis, Nice, Corsica, Savoy!" and advancing into the streets with posters demanding France surrender Tunisia, Savoy, and Corsica to Italy. The French premier, Edouard Daladier, rapidly rejected the Italian request for concessions to territorial rights as France as well as Italy were at the edge of war during the majority of the winter from 1938 to 39.

Mussolini got his information from British Premier Neville Chamberlain's view to Rome during the month of January 1939. Britain was really seeking better relationships with Italy and desired to reach concessions, it was not going to cut off all relations with France in the interest of an even stronger Anglo-Italian partnership.

This is why Mussolini became more interested in Germany's idea of an alliance with the army, which he first found out about in the month of May. Mussolini spoke to members of the Fascist Grand Council in the period of February 1939 where he proclaimed his conviction that the state's powers are limited "Italy was considered a "detainee within the Mediterranean and the larger and more powerful Italy is in the future, the more likely it is to suffer from its prison time," according to the report. Corsica, Tunisia, Malta and Cyprus are the bars of the jail; Gibraltar and Suez are the jail's guards "

The change in course was not without being spotted by opposition. Italo Balbo accused Mussolini in "licking Hitler's boot" at a meeting that was held at the Fascist Grand Council on March 21st 1939. Balbo condemned the Duce's pro-German diplomatic policy for dragging Italy towards disaster, while considering his assertion that "opening of the door to Britain" continued to exist and allying with Germany was not a necessity. Even though some gerarchi, such as Balbo did not support closer ties to Berlin but Mussolini's dominance of foreign-politics equipment meant the issues of these gerarchi were not addressed. In Balbo's rant against Mussolini to blame him for "licking Hitler's feet" and his demand that"opening to Britain" be done "opening for Britain" was resisted in the meeting that was held by the Fascist Grand Council, and the Greek journalist Aristotle Kallis called

Mussolini's "fairly moderate" reactions show that his reaction was surprisingly restrained. Nazi Party had absolutely nothing like that of the Fascist Grand Council, and it was impossible to imagine that any of the Hitland's chiefs would feel with this. Mussolini directed the invasion into Albania during March 1939. Albania was devastated by Italy within just five days, requiring the King Zog to abandon the country and establishing the period of Italian government in Albania. The Axis was not fully established until May 1939 however, that month witnessed the finalization of the Pact of Steel, which described the "friendship and cooperation" among Germany as well as Italy and was signed by all of the foreign ministers of both countries. This Pact of Steel was a military alliance that was simultaneously infuriating and defensive. Mussolini did not sign it until following the issuance of a promise by his fellow Germans to ensure there'd not be war over the next three years. Italy's king

Victor Emanuel the Third was also sceptical of the agreement and opted for more conventional Italian allies like France and was frightened by consequences of an offensive alliance between the army, which ultimately resulted in the transfer of control over the peace and war to Hitler.

Chapter 6: Mussolini's Early Years

It's difficult to remember the young age Italy was at the time that Benito Mussolini was born on July 29th 1883. It's difficult to comprehend that the country that has such a lengthy and historical past was not once so young, and plagued by continuous conflict and instabilities. Like Germany, Italy was unified in 1861. But, as opposed like its northern neighbor it had a previous one of division. Italy was not a dream of an "Great Germany,"" maintaining its unity through wars between the city states. 1 Benito Mussolini was born and was raised in a unstable environment, where concepts that were thought to be extreme by the majority of modern observers, including Socialism that would go through an intense and brutal transformation.

His family was wealthy according to Italian standards at the time however, they were in the midst of scandal and had to dispose of their entire land to pay off their obligations.

As one of the first Italian Socialists His father was a proponent of an idealism that was reminiscent to be an anarchist who was extreme. His arrests were numerous however his standing protected him from the repercussions. Although the young Benito was awed by the political activities of his father but it his mother, who was a Catholic both politically and religiously she brought peace for the family that which his father was unable to support. The mother also gave him all of his educational needs. [2]

The Mussolini's youthful years were a mix of radical politics and extreme. The Italian was known to be aggressive and susceptible to over alcohol consumption. Between 1892-1894, Benito was involved in a string of heinous acts, and was expelled from an institution called a Salesian college after stabbing the other student. This is a testimony to the turbulent period in Italy that, despite all these issues the fact that not only did Benito complete his studies in the year 1901, however, less than a an year later, the entrepreneur was instructing in a rural institution located in Gualtieri, a town in Gualtieri.

Mussolini was a member of his fellow members of the Italian Socialist party in 1900 and emigrated to Switzerland in 1902, attempting to escape being drafted into the army. This may appear unusual, when you consider that the fact that it was taken by someone who was not just a leader of the Italian military, but would have an ideology that was filled with military ideology and war-mongering. In order to understand the reasoning behind his choice one must be realized that the beginning of the twentieth century Italian Army was a very restrictive and politically-repressive institution. For many, escaping from the service was, for a lot of openly involved political leaders an option to not be scolded for their political views within a military that was known for its strict use of physical discipline.

Mussolini was a victim of two years of absolute misery. Although he could provide for himself by physical labor however, the self-imposed isolation caused mental stress to his condition. In these times the fervent anticlericalism of his became into a radical view. The speeches he delivered, in which he demanded God to exist and to attack him wherever the he was standing-- caused the issue of scandal. However, military service was an obligation that was not to be snubbed. Swiss authorities quickly became irritated over Mussolini's political stance and reacted swiftly by detaining him, and then transferring his body to Italian officials. Luck was on his side as, in 1904 Mussolini was scheduled to stand trial for defiance however he was granted amnesty. which was granted to commemorate the birth of a new prince Umberto. Prince Umberto.

The identification card of Mussolini after he was detained in 1903

When he was first admitted to the military unit in which he had to continue his duty-- Mussolini remained strict in order to stay out of the repercussions of his earlier political involvement. His opportunity to escape the "undesirables" occurred with the loss of his mother in 1905. In the wake of this sad time, Mussolini wrote a profoundly patriotic letter to his bosses and gained their confidence through a mix of ideological and emotional manipulative. It was his ability to "go along with the flow" and make use of any circumstance to his advantage and give his beliefs if needed the fundamental beliefs the man had been steadfastly defending until the moment of his death were crucial aspects of his personality. This would not only affect his life, but also the whole history of the Italian nation. 3 At the time, Mussolini was a Socialist and a fervent believer in the teachings of Marx, but he also mingled with violent attitudes as well as a deep disdain towards the rule of law. He saw it as an obstacle between his and the outcome the he wished for. 4. Drawing a complete historical compass for Mussolini's political existence is difficult, as his views varied according to the circumstances and environment. Although a glance at his face may be revealing a person who was agnostic but was open to changing his views according to his needs A different viewpoint could show someone who is troubled, looking to find something in between nationalist beliefs as well as general Socialism.

In the years 1906-1909 Mussolini taught at the school of Tolmezzo the town of Tolmezzo, which is located in Northern Italy, and his social activism returned and increased by engaging in activities that were based outside of Italy including anticlerical activity within Trento located deep within Austrian territory.

The new peaceful stage in my life as a teacher, was short time. The year 1911 was the time when Italy entered Libya in an effort to become part of the international community, and benefit from the advantages of an empire that was colonial. Mussolini quickly jumped into the cause. Although his political activities were linked to his anti-war inclinations but his main goal was to mobilize the population into a violent Socialist movement against the ruling class. This was an unattainable idea he pursued using whatever it was imaginable to do during time time and that included street-level protests and public speaking. He was detained on the night of the 14th of October, 1911 being accused of "sabotaging the efforts of war" and sentenced to one year in prison. He utilized that time to draft anti-clerical documents that he could use in subsequent events in the political arena. The fact that slamming Catholic beliefs and doctrines in Italy during that time was viewed as more a an act of political rage than a religious discussion due to the fact that the Catholic church had a substantial influence over the majority of the populace.

Mussolini in the 1900s

The Socialist Party

Jail time was a way to provide Mussolini with some recognition in The National Socialist Party, granting him an enviable position in 1912 the more moderate section of the organization was thrown out. This made room for the radical and new faces. Mussolini was appointed the post as chief editor for Avanti! magazine, and was a well-known political Italian voice through the magazine's pages. Following the takeover of Avanti! In 1913, Mussolini continued to push for a radical revolution against the government that, according to his eyes, not bringing back majority of the people and only focusing on making it easier for wealthy capitalists. Mussolini advocated for the creation of a "bloodbath," and the "physical elimination" of bourgeoisie his writings. Although a small portion of the Socialist Party considered Mussolini's views radical and unproductive The majority believed that he was in the midst of a revolution that was violent, prepared to fight and take what they thought was theirs. [5]

The rise of radical socialism with strong determination slowly escalated tensions and culminated in a rage during 1914 with a series of violent protests known by the name of Red Week, that shook Italy to the heart. They were not part of any coordinated plan rather a spontaneous eruption of anger at a regime that proved insensitive to the majority of social issues and vulnerable to violent repression as well as the total defense of the status of the game. Due to his past of violence it is reasonable to think that Mussolini would be right comfortable in this type of setting, however being able to learn from his mistakes, he largely abstained from the protests by merely reading the pages from Avanti!. The disastrous Red Week Revolution, easily suppressed by the state, gave Mussolini the importance of a insight: popular rebellion wasn't a viable route towards success. To find a better way to be in power, Mussolini will soon leave his political group.

The start of the First World War left Italy in a precarious spot. Although Italy was not a party to the war or compelling reasons for joining in the conflict, because the defense alliance agreement with the central powers held little significance following the time that Germany began to go in the offensive and a heated internal discussion was brewing. It was clear that neutrality for the Socialists was a direct challenge by those who believed that taking part in the war as the only option to retake the last natural Italian territory to be reclaimed from Austria including Trieste, the capital city. Trieste. Mussolini was the first to start his campaign, he followed strict Socialist policy through Avanti however, in the month of September, 1914, he started an escalating series of private gatherings with the members of the other side. Sixteenth of October in the same year Avanti! published an article that emphasized active neutrality, as opposed to total neutrality. This was an attempt to encourage cooperating with the forces of intervention and eventually the conflict in itself. Although this may seem like to be a minor difference in language however, it was clear that the Socialist Party took it extremely serious. After publishing his piece, Mussolini was expelled from his group. Within a few months and he was already the editor of the publication Popolo d'Italia, which encouraged Italy to join the war.

Exiled by being a part of the Socialist Party was a risk however Mussolini was able to comprehend his place in the political landscape and all of the elements at play throughout Italian political life. The left, primarily represented through the Socialist Party, was not capable of coordinating the violent revolution that was part of Mussolini's vision, but is also averse to his specific style of leadership, which is more like that of a war commander as opposed to an intellectual. Mussolini was more suited to benefit from the side of intervention and its propagandistic and nationalist propaganda. As a supporter of war his supporters included majority of the elite and upper middle class that provided his with significant finances. Mussolini was the Socialist Party's greatest nightmare. He was a Popolo d'Italia was capable of reaching out to the lower classes with similar slogans and terms while promoting a message that was warmth rather than the universal neutrality that the Socialists believed in.

When Popolo d'Italia was now recognized as one of the Socialist Party's most dangerous opposition politicians, Mussolini kept repeating that the man was a fervent Socialist even when they did not consider him an individual. It is important to point to be noted that if one considers the fact that his specific line of Socialism was firmly rooted in anarchist views, this might be taken as a factual statement but it's the case that when he shifted into the direction of intervention the practical side of his mind, always looking for new ways to increase his influence, gradually dissociating him from the old ways of thinking. Mussolini was the first to push his idea to enter the war on the basis of material gain and reclaiming what was thought to be Italian country, then growing into Dalmatia as well as Dalmatia and the Middle East. The entire intervening side, including Mussolini in particular -- wanted to make clear how much material gain could be made with the thought of an the simplest and shortest conflict. Other motives of ideology were in playing more than that. The major powers that were already combating the Italian nationalists wanted the opportunity to demonstrate themselves by undergoing the thrilling experience that war was intended to be like, and also to put all notions and concepts of the patriotic into practice and make themselves heroes as the men who unified Italy. If the politician changed sides and left his former political party Mussolini was not able to change his methods. His brutality was the primary focus of numerous writings that were published in 1915. Sometimes, they even threatened with a call to overthrow the monarchy in the event that Italy did not join the conflict at an most extreme. Cowardice was not an option under Mussolini's political rhetoric, and staying away from what was believed to be the biggest and most lucrative conflict during Italian time time was not acceptable.

World War I

Italy made a decision to fight and joined the war on May 24 1915, with the assurance in the secret London pact every desired territory along the borders of the north and Balkans were to become Italian following the Austrians lost. Italy fell into war, pushed by numerous forces, but at the top of government, a lot did not believe in the interventionist stance, believing the neutrality of the country would turn out more beneficial. The Italian middle class rose and marched into battle exactly as they and their German and French predecessors prior to their time. An entire century of love between middle-classes was lost in the First World War, wrote Francis Scott Fitzgerald decades later in his book Tender is the Night, providing readers with one of the most concise descriptions of the fervor that led generation after generation out of home and university and to the battlefields. Mussolini was drafted into the army as part of his class of age on the 31st of August 1915 as a corporal however, his Socialist connection prevented him from attending the officer school at where he wanted to go. This was a standard working procedure for an army under absolute conservatism, and where loyalty or affiliation to Socialist beliefs was not acceptable.

Mussolini encountered political hurdles throughout the course of his World War I experience, yet his inherent violent stance and the ability to adjust to the most extreme circumstances resulted in him being a superb soldier who was and was praised by his commanders. Mussolini never lost sight of his political goals throughout the war, and constantly tried to improve his standing in spite of being confined to the trenches. He kept a day-to- journal of his war experiences that returned in his Popolo d'Italia for publication, showing himself not as an army hero, but as an impressive leader working to unify the nation away out of the trenches, where various social classes merged into one entity. [8]

The Mussolini's "great war" experiences were crucial, in a variety of ways, to his eventual political rise and ascendance to the top of the political ladder and should be something is worth spending time in defining. The Italian front there were the latest technological advances and tactics across all fronts, in which the combination of artillery and barbed wire could transform the notion of the romantic and noble war into an incredibly terrifying experience one of the closest things the human race has ever witnessed to hell in the earth. It was the Italian front was situated on the Eastern Alps and included some of the highest mountains of Europe. Soldiers battled from peak to peak staying in caves and pushing supplies over the treacherous slopes. 9 On the 23rd of September in 1917 Mussolini was wounded in multiple ways following shrapnel in a rogue wave. The most obvious consequence of the incident was the abolition of his participation directly during the war, it is also the moment that his narcissistic tendencies were brought into the spotlight. When he wrote Popolo d'Italia, he wrote about his alleged decision to refusing painkillers when medical personnel took shrapnel off his body. It is true it was because Mussolini was always dramatic when he wrote but this marked the start of a style that would be the norm for the rest of his existence, since his work was never-ending to give a dazzling dramatic, epic feeling to the.

After the fighting, Mussolini found Popolo d'Italia facing a huge financial crisis. Although this could be a challenge in his standing and capacity to address the nation but in reality the mission had accomplished, and the issues had nothing to do with the future of Mussolini as a political public figure. The proof was in the fact that rather than reeking of the most extreme of his speech to lure investors into moderately sized companies and investors, he continued to accuse government officials of not fighting for the victory in a sufficient manner, and at the same time condemning the censorship of military officials. With the assistance of the right-wing disappearing, Mussolini made a small gesture of reuniting with a few old Socialist Party acquaintances. It's not clear how this could affect the course of Italian politics, since the biggest fight during World War I was being conducted in the Italian front at the time the letters were sent between the two sides, trampled every political sphere.

The 24th day of October 1917, at a region in the Italian front, dubbed Caporetto and the German Army's reinforcements the German Army to which the Austrians have been waiting was delivered. The Italians were fighting in bloody combat against the weak and demoralized remains of an empire dying and were confronted by an army that was the strongest to ever be seen as they were amazed. Although the war was ended militarily with the reorganization of an army on the River Piave, such a devastating defeat could have lasting implications in the political sphere. This is all in the favor of the people who, as Mussolini and others, who had criticised the war effort and had a firm "warrior-like" philosophy. Prior to Caporetto, Mussolini had pushed for a more aggressive approach, condemning the government for not allowing using the "terrorist strikes" against German cities. In the event that the prospect of losing began to become a reality the rhetoric of his opponent found new ears and contributed to the development of his "legendary" politics.

Mussolini was employed to aid the Italian government to take on the powerful campaign for neutrality from the Socialists. Once peace was signed Mussolini was put to rest indefinitely, and not to be seen on the center of Italian public life. After the conclusion of the First World War, Italy was a completely different place with a completely different culture that the traditional and traditional political elite could not comprehend. Mussolini had now found himself in a society where violence and revolution were able to slash down one of the great old monarchies of Russia and where the experiences of soldiers during the war united an once divided Italian population; and the country of Italy in which the government and military had launched a massive campaign to build the concept of an Italian country's identity and to increase its use of the country's principal Italian language. In the aftermath of conflict, Italy was filled with veterans who returned home to bring their new ideas and new experiences, all ready to put their newly acquired combat skills to help a reason.

Mussolini in 1917

The Bolshevik Revolution wasn't just important as it demonstrated the possibility of overthrowing old government. The Bolsheviks published the numerous secret agreements kept under the Tsarist monarchy. They showed that materialism and imperialism are the main reasons for the wars of all nations. A treaty of this kind that was mentioned before, the London Pact, revealed what was promises to Italy in order to make people realize the extent to which Italy was not won to the point of defeat. Italy wasn't awarded Trieste nor the Dalmatian territory. The reason for this is complicated and go into the world of the world of international politics, which is a far cry away from our subject. The most important thing is that the vast majority of people -- from veterans to families of those who suffered the loss of everything they had during the war, began to feel like they were taken advantage of by the rest of the world. It was as the sacrifices they made, as well as their deaths, had gone unnoticed when other nations enjoyed the celebration of triumph. A fear of the new Communist danger and hatred of"mutilated victory "Mutilated Victory" affected many people, preparing to be manipulated by those who claimed they supported war but were critical of the state since the very beginning. If the ruling class was ready to eliminate Mussolini out as a leader, he was placed the ideal candidate to lead an entirely new movement that was unlike anything previously seen.

Chapter 7: A New Prime Minister

Although Mussolini as well as others Italian authors and politicians utilized every trick from the book to spread outrage over the ending of the war across people, the motives for this reaction lay in reality. Italy was greatly affected by the famous Fourteen Points, his philosophy to autonomy. However, at the similar time that the more powerful power was dividing the globe in accordance with the imperialistic logic that was that was not confined to Europe. Italy was regarded as an inferior power, and was sacrificed to its "altar" of matters deemed more important. [11]

It's easy to track this rise in the fury by studying the number of readers. When the financial situation was incredibly difficult that year, the journal was able to sell 60,000 copies per day, but it should be noted that the accounting records show Popolo d'Italia earned eight times greater than in the year before. [12]

In the midst of the increasing popularity of his image, Mussolini chose to finally be a political leader instead of being a activist or a journalist. The 23rd March, 1919, before a small group of less than one hundred persons, made up of former Socialists, Anarchists, republicans and liberals, he laid the initial core in the Fascist Party.

The radical ideology of the fascist demanded a total state revolution, far more than the current socialists and called for the removal of the monarchy in an entirely new republic, giving farmland directly to farmers and imposing a substantial tax on big capitals as well as inheritances, nationalizing industries and placing it under the directly supervised control of the state as well as granting women with voting rights. [13]

The document was strikingly identical to the principles of Socialism. The manifesto also separated its members from the movement specifically due to its ferocious opposing Socialism in itself. On the 15th of April 1919

Members of the new Fascist militants violently attacked the l'Avanti! office, a Socialist magazine for which Mussolini was chief editor. Although he wasn't directly involved during the riot however, he did refer to it as the beginning of the Fascist revolution's victory. Mussolini became a hero of all who resisted the conservative current government and those and conservatives, but without the label of Socialist in any way, and also people who wanted not just the opposite political perspective, but also a social revolution. In November 19, 1919, Mussolini was elected to the Italian parliament in Milan with the radical anti-clerical, anti-socialist role as the mainstay for his victory. The result was disastrous for Mussolini. Socialists got nearly 50 percent of his vote, but Mussolini was completely defeated.

Mussolini when he was working as a l'Avanti employee. l'Avanti!

After the results of the election after the election, the government clamped down against him and his organization as a police search took place in at the Popolo d'Italia offices and found many explosives and weapons, a clear evidence of the movement's violence. The day was supposed to be Mussolini's final date with the political system, but instead the politician was detained and released immediately without charge.

This could be the start of a tolerance policy which is difficult to understand without understanding the backdrop of the complete terror of Socialism and, more specifically, Communism. Mussolini and the Fascists he allied with could be saved due to having in mind that their primary goal for their violent actions were precisely the enemies that they were fighting. This was due to the fact that the identical enemies had recently gained a victory in the polls, and had gained a place in the state which scared the regime to equip him with all the weapons at his arsenal, even the Fascists.

Demoralized and with diminishing number of supporters--which was just 4000 at the time of his first election of the year 1920 -- Mussolini was waiting for his opportunity. It came in the years 1920-1921 as the "Socialist threat" began to rise up in an attempt to take over the industry and the production methods. The years, commonly referred to as"the "two red years" were characterized as the ensuing protests and strikes led by Socialists as well as Communists that were large enough to scare the older elite, but not enough to overthrow the government. 14) The Fascists instantly found themselves back in their homes, and transformed into the brutal arm of Conservative reactions, and then forming Literal commandos. These were known in the form of "Squadre in azione" (action squads). They were rendered extremely risky due to the presence of veteran soldiers who endorsed Mussolini's views and were pushed into action due to Socialist initiatives. A lot of prominent people from the financial and industrial world started to offer Fascist groups to protect themselves since they had a tremendously effective way of the dismantling and breaking up strikes using brutal force. Through all this turmoil and chaos, the Fascist group was in danger of becoming a number of diverse bands, each with its own local leadership. Only because of Mussolini's capacity to change and communicate what was right for the correct people, and alter his views according to the needs of his followers that he managed to preserve a certain unity within the group. The 2nd Fascist Congress on May 25 of 1920 Mussolini dropped his Republican decision and made his support for the wealthy. Considering the Fascists to be their most effective weapon against the "red danger," the Italian government eventually decided to recognize the existence of their politically powerful force.

This led to the Mussolini's eventual being elected to the Italian the Italian Parliament. Support from the government, direct support from the government, weaponry, and guaranteed security from legal consequences were provided to the squadre of the Azione. In 1921, Mussolini -- believed to be a member of the elite--trained them as well as assisting their opponents in the field, while criticizing their decisions as insensitive or incoherent. The result was slowly building the "strong man" reputation. The very first Fascist Parliamentary faction wasn't the only party he had but was a part of the Liberal right in their electoral lists. They were chosen through an extraordinary usage of violence in politics on Election Day. Voters were assaulted and/or assaulted when they went in and out of polling stations if they refused to declare that they voted for Fascist candidates. Parliamentarians were repeatedly beaten and intimidated or (in cases like socialist Giuseppe di Valgno) executed with the help of Squadre d'azione. Mussolini was able to create a frightening beast and allowed it to terrorize not just those who were "reds," but all Italian political parties. He was the sole person who was in control of its reigns, shooting it where he liked. When he was on the ground the commandos he had commanded strayed from the laws as he governed an authentic political group that gained the respect of people who were awed by those who were being beat and kept an unassuming image when it came to moderate Conservatives.

Surprised and shocked, the Liberal political elite gradually retreated against Fascist brutality. Between 1921 until 1922, the entire public was crippled in the wake of an unexpected taking over. In the month of August, 1922 the Socialists began to stand and take control of the state by staging a huge protest and fighting for the restoration of the law of the land. Mussolini could not have wished for a better scenario. The

Fascist movement was awash with Socialist activity because many of them were afraid of leftists doing anything even remotely similar to a revolutionary movement, in particular because they were more coordinated to fight in the streets, street by street. [15] The Squadre di'azione launched a gang that was completely free of restrictions fight against strikers and the Socialist party in all its aspects. Between September and October Mussolini had formulated his plans for an absolute, total overthrow, stating, "They'll surrender the state either way, or we'll conquer it with a march on Rome."[1616

The 27th of October, 1922 the threat was real. With the support of mass of the public, Fascist commandos moved toward Rome and Mussolini was in Milan waiting for the government's, and specifically, the king's response. The government quickly asked the for the King of Italy Vittorio Emanuele III to sign a decree which authorized the use by troops to stop the unconstitutional march, however the request was denied.

The King was of the opinion that a lot of his army members sympathized with Mussolini and his side and that should he order the troops to stop them then they would turn their backs on the monarchy, turning an opposition to the government into a marches against the state and eventually taking away the King's power. Between getting rid of Mussolini and keeping his position, Vittorio Emanuele III chose the second option. Although it's easy to imagine Mussolini as a spider within the web of King's power, flawlessly moving to take over power but one must remember his youthfulness and specific abilities and not be influenced by the success of the operation. A transcript of a meeting that took place on the 28th of October 1922 portray Mussolini as uncertain of how to proceed and being forced by Fascist leaders to take over power. Mussolini was not the most decisive figure in the face of a crisis. However, his ability was there, just after the political direction was decided to follow the line and to play the game very well.

The March on Rome conflict ended prior to any Fascist-related group made it to Rome, the capital. At the time they arrived Rome, Mussolini had already received the mandate to establish the new government. He could therefore be able to portray himself as a hero of triumph before his people and treat the people as a warrior army that had conquered. When he was 40, Mussolini became the youngest premier in Italian history. He embarked on the long and difficult process to form his own government with the help of the capitalist forces that were present in Italy and was happy to know to know that an Fascist administration would mean complete suppression of Socialist actions. Within a short time, Fascism had transformed from the tiniest movement of a hundred or so people in a small room to a major social movement that was followed by thousands as well as an encroaching academic group of intellectuals.

Mussolini in the march on Rome

Mussolini had created his own political system, however it was still minority in the vast right-wing alliance of Liberals, Democrats, Nationalists, Catholics, independents, and even members of the military who were in the majority of executive power. The fact that he was a minority kept the majority of the nation's elite confident they were only in an inflection point, a part of the anti-Socialist program which was to shortly return to normal. But, Mussolini and the other Fascist officials saw beyond the simplistic notion of playing the state bear, as a way to gain authority. For him, this means that he can continue playing until the last struggle or authority outside of the Fascist party was wiped out. The 16th of November 1922

Mussolini and his high-pitched voice inside their chamber, informed members of parliament that he had the power to crush all of the structure if wanted to and had been governing the system of old with his benevolent will which could shift anytime. [17]

His experience as a foreign politician that began when he was apprehensive and had very little to speak of in the world stage started in 1922. In Italy the declarations depicted Mussolini as a solution to international issues but in actual fact, Mussolini had no experience with these issues. Outside of Italy there was no power for the Fascists were not able to utilize, but within the territory of Italy, Squadre d'Azione activities were enhanced by their leader appointed Premier. While the violence served in the short time, Mussolini knew it could not continue unchecked or ultimately, be the allies of theirs, who were happy with the Fascists' ability to keep Socialists down--against.

The first step was to change the Squadre d'Azione to a volunteer militia under his direct control and becoming a part of the government. It meant that Fascist activities were directly linked to its more legitimate political branches and was forced to get caught up in the extremes. Although this was certainly not well-appreciated by his supporters however, the establishment of the Fascist Grand Council (Gran Consiglio of Fascismo) as the governing part of the party offered several leaders from "commando" teams a clear route to the top. In the end, after gaining full control over his own party, Mussolini also began the slow process of getting total control over the government. As one of the clearest violations of his principles Mussolini reverted to the foundational beliefs of his youth to strengthen his ties with the Conservatives and endorsed legislation that was favored by the Vatican. Mussolini--who suffered hardships in favor of voicing his anti-clericalism--finally aligned himself with those he hated to guarantee a stronger hold on power.

With the ability to control practically all of the country, but with just a small fraction of the House at a level of parliamentary representation, Mussolini rectified this problem in 1923, on the 21st July through the adoption of an infamous set of laws for the upcoming elections. He also granted two-thirds the House to the group which was able to secure greater than 25% of votes.

However, even if Mussolini had begun to abandon his street gangs in 1924, the election in 1924 witnessed an unprecedented amount of violence. It was never considered to be as a possibility, and defeat was impossible as the Fascist organizations were able to maintain control over polling locations throughout the election. After every vote was taken into account in what was considered as the most secluded elections ever in Italian time in the past, the Fascist group won the election with more than 65% of votes. One Socialist politician dared voice his displeasure about the outcome within the parliament, and it is Giacomo Matteotti. In the speech--in which he pointed out many irregularities--Matteotti said that with his words he was condemning himself to death. The next day the words he spoke of became the reality of a brutal, crude act after an Fascist organization Mussolini could have protected him against legal consequences kidnapped and executed his body. [18]

Matteotti

It's impossible to determine whether Mussolini specifically ordered the murder however it is well-known that he made similar orders to the police in several instances like the murder of Pietro Gobetti, for which the written and signed orders was uncovered. Following the news that Matteotti was murdered, Mussolini tried to cover his murder by thinking that he may have fled and escaped to South America. The Italian denied any knowledge of the matter, and even secured the murderers through assigning a portion of his party for the probe.

Mussolini might have believed that Matteotti's remains would not be discovered and be found, but after Matteotti was discovered, Italy awoke from its sleeping slumber only to be afflicted by violence and the total lack of law. The majority of Liberals left the Fascist causes, and an outpouring of discontent and rage was emitted by those who were politically educated. The 27th of June 1924 The political opposition, which included lawmakers that were not members of the Fascist party -- decided to leave the chamber and withdraw to protest. The crisis profoundly affected Mussolini emotionally and physically. But a myriad of circumstances made him a powerful politician. In this crucial point, opposition leaders proved not to be able to stand up for themselves through general strikes. Although the King and Vatican have backed Mussolini but the former believed that he was able to control the Fascists far better than any other party as well as the latter wanted to pressure the newly-established majority party into making more concessions. On paper, this seemed like a dangerous time due to Mussolini's continuous struggle for the powerhouse opposition members were never sufficient to coordinate an effective retaliation against Mussolini. The Socialists were the sole one who could take on the Fascists in the field as well as their opponents, the Liberals were the political party that had used the Fascists against them over the last five years. The only force that could challenge Mussolini -- at most if the troops followed his directives was the King because he remained the an absolute military commander, but the political opposition Mussolini had to face was created and largely by those that wanted nothing more than to remove his authority and transform Italy into one of two republics or a Socialist nation. It wasn't just the finality of Mussolini however, it was a ferocious aggressive, violent and despotic movement that would eliminate freedom of speech, press as well as the freedom of speech and even the right to protest.

In the years 1925-1926 between 1925 and 1926, the Italian state was rebuilt through a string of laws that smashed the democratic system of the country, and creating the new dictatorial regimes. A lot of opposition figures were blasted on the streets, while the state-run Socialist Party was made an unlawful entity, and was removed from public life. Private lives too were changed when Mussolini disbanded the majority of organisations and organizations that had legal merit as well as removing his opponents' the ability to gather privately under the lawful veil of anonymity. Every activity was scrutinized and Informers and spies were brought to justice in the most prestigious social levels, while the vast majority of magazines and newspapers were confiscated or dismantled. In the midst of all this many attempted in physically eliminating Mussolini and he resisted every attempt, but he became more aware of his perilous circumstance, where a wrong move could end up costing the man his life.

At the close of 1926 the parties had all been disbanded except for those of the Fascist one. The strategy of Mussolini was to be an anaconda, and carefully stifle resistance from the entirety of Italian society by imposing Fascist control over every aspect of life. In the beginning, many attempted to get rid of the dictator, the plan was successful, and with time Mussolini would soon return to a more peaceful life style, deemed to be the latest political fact by many, while those opposed to it were pushed underground and waited to be given a opportunity. Today, Mussolini had Italy in his grasp, with only the hefty cost on the state was in front of his back. In the course of his last period in the advance towards to the Second World War, it may be clear that something's not quite right the ability to define the definition of what Fascism was. Mussolini moved between Socialism as well as capitalistic connections anti-clericalism, as well as Republicanism and what fascists at the time was a nationalism-based, reactionary organization, mostly operating in opposition to the law of.

The initial days of the Fascist administration were marked by the efforts of Mussolini to improve his reputation both within as well as outside the country. Within the context of his Fascist Party, he managed to gradually incorporate many options, like one of the most prominent future-oriented leaders who were who could provide a comparable right-wing agenda. In the world the party was able to secure a modest success in the negotiation of adding Fiume, the city Fiume in Italy's northern frontier. Though it was not significant from a business perspective but it was a way for Mussolini could show himself to the veterans who were angry at the conclusion in World War I as the one who had secured the victory to their "greedy of the hands" of the great nations. The Italian also began to prepare for an upcoming push to establish the status of an Italian colonial empire using his experience in the Roman Empire as his main image of propagandism and the reconstruction as the main goal he wanted to show the world.

Mussolini was accustomed to his methods of working with his Italian populace, one that was who was caught in a state of development between a pure agriculture-based country and a more modern country. As he began to employ similar methods in other colonial areas, such Somalia, which was already being under Italian command, he realized that the results were quite distinct. While traveling through the Somalia colony in 1926 Mussolini arrived at the helm of two ironclads as well as 15 other warships. It was a show of force designed to calm angry inhabitants. While he was unable to stop the unending guerrilla assaults of the people, Mussolini discovered they were prepared to accept the threat. In the aftermath of his visit, situation deteriorated and it was never completely peaceful. As all of it was in preparation for the Ethiopian assault, it's not difficult to see the strategy of international Fascist political stances--aggression at its purest shape, with the aim of making their nation into the huge strong entity that they believed it to be. minds, meant to be. Politics within the internal, on side, however, were improving.

Intellectuals of the Fascist elite, as well as Mussolini himself were creating an entire body of work, with precise definitions of the essence of what Fascism was. The state, which was the only party system, was at the source of everything. In the framework of Fascism, Mussolini had his time to shine as everything had to go through the rigid state control. In contrast with Socialism the goal of Fascism was not to "socialize the production process," but to "socialize individuals," creating a new Italian man who was a fierce soldier for his country, always in touch with the state from birth until the time of his death. A person would be born, and join in the Balilla Organization, the Fascist youth association, and then his work would be overseen through the Fascist "corporation." The man's interests would be governed by the Fascist association and sports would be facilitated by Fascist organisations, and the news by way of Fascist publications. The approach of the Fascist economics was not as than ideological. When, at one time, Mussolini and the Fascist elite attempted to establish an "third economic alternative" that was a compromise between Communism and Capitalism by establishing organisations that were reminiscent of the medieval "guilds," each one focused on controlling a particular part of the industrial and economic life, it never led to any real changes. Mussolini was always adamant about his loyalty to capitalist investors which was one of the very few groups of people that he could not stop without grave economic consequences. Mussolini stated Fascism on the 26th of May 1927 in an address before the Italian parliament "Everything within the state and nothing that is not against the state, and nothing that is not a part of the State."

While his initial international gatherings were greeted by great powerhouses with coldness and disinterest, when he took over the entire power, certain prominent political leaders began to look his way and respect. In January 1927 Winston Churchill praised him and his "victory over the Leninist desires" in his trip to Rome. In the realm of culture, based on the concept of "socializing individuals," Fascism began pushing strict limits and clearly defined that emphasized the leader of the state as its primary goal. Between 1929 between 1931 and 1929, Mussolini collaborated with writer Giovacchino Forzano in the production of two dramatic works from the past. His love of drama that he displayed in his rise to power was a mainstay of his personality, pushing him into projects that did not fit his "Strong the warrior-hero" persona.

The effects that are direct from all these actions are hard to measure since they had radically different results from a different perspective. Intellectuals who opposed Fascism maintained their work by holding secret meetings and slowly creating a works. Particularly, those who were Socialists as well as Communists which would significantly influence European left-wing groups for decades ahead, but people of all ages were at risk of being influenced by the tactics of Mussolini. As time passed, more and more people came to trust in the propaganda machine for culture produced. It was time to be Mussolini allies since this ubiquitous Fascist actions impacted the whole globe, and a generation of children could develop, and in some instances were forever scarred after having been conditioned from the age of a child. It was the "Duce," title used by Mussolini when he assumed total supreme control over the state, was always correct and adherence to his dictates was the only way to be a servant to the state.

The power of the state has changed Mussolini in every way starting with his appearance. His typical middle-class attire was changed to numerous army uniforms. He was able to improve his public image by meticulously showing his athleticism as well as performing hard physical farming as often as was possible. The Duce was required to be a an enthralling, magnificent figure as well as a an integral part of the community that he governed; as a farmer and warrior, in a way that was as free of the stale, aging state-sponsored thugs who were a part of Italian political life prior to his rise as was possible. Mussolini was finally able to move from Rome in 1928. Rome in 1928 along with his wife Rachele as well as his daughters and two sons.

The subject we've been discussing till now, the notion of all things existing within the state was the aim of Mussolini's Fascist movement. However, like Hitler as well as Stalin, Mussolini never achieved his dreams. Generations that grew in the era of his dictatorship included Fascists and anti-Fascists. But the majority of the Italian populace was uninterested and dwelling in communities and villages, where politics included their less skilled local officials. A large part of the failure to carry out his plan could be blamed on the state structure it self, because Mussolini was a co-ruler with two other organizations. One was the King, who was commander-in-chief of the military, who in silence supported his agenda, yet could, theoretically in theory, to eliminate him from his position. The other was the Church that remained in power, and had an enormous power over the people and had the ability to counter the Fascist dominant culture. [22]

Naturally, Mussolini didn't leave the Democratic structure unaltered. The rules of the past were changed and that was why the Fascist Party remained the only lawful entity to exist. Furthermore, elections were made insignificant since the only authority of voters was to approve or reject an electoral list that included 400 potential applicants for Parliament. Ministers, who were once a symbol of the government as well as the political parties that formed it became administrators with the power to dismiss or hire. Mussolini could dismiss or hire according to his own discretion, decisions typically were made using the same hard-headed style of thinking he had followed throughout his existence. The structure created an increasing amount of accountability at the control of the Duce who, for the longest time, depended on external assistance to determine the proper path to take in politics. Mussolini began to surround himself with loyalists rather than the most knowledgeable.

Ten years after the march into Rome the 27th of October in 1932, Mussolini continued to repeat much of what he had ordered in the previous ten years that the country should be more fascist and the Italian population needed to make changes, and this was done through violence, if needed. After reading the declarations, one would expect to see a huge range of political decisions needed for putting the Fascist programme into effect However, just following the 10th anniversary Mussolini rather signed an enormous amnesty that pardoned several of the people suspected of conspiring against his government. The events illustrate the traits Mussolini consistently displayed throughout his earlier years that he was constantly fighting in battle after fight, and then fight, systematically pursuing an end was a challenge for him and he always chose the least effort.

Chapter 8: War In Africa

The Italian public was different from the other European populace in its views of the grand European imperial venture. Only under Mussolini's regime that an influx of nationalist sentiment and an intense patriotic sentiments ignited the flames on the Italian imperial flame. Before then it was Italy was Italian state was, at a certain point emerged from its own history of colonization. Having been administered and occupied as fragmented entities mainly by Spain as well as Austria.

In the similar time it was also true that the inspiring rhetoric around Risorgimento tried to bring back memories of the origins of Italy's history within the era of Rome and its past the glory of imperial rule was one aspect which Italians across different dialects and ideologies could be in agreement on. For a nation to be powerful and be considered a serious player in the European scene the country had to be a part of an empire with colonies. Ultimately, few agreed on this.

In addition colonies can be used in order to alleviate the over populace, and channel the crippling exodus of Italy to other countries filled with possibilities, yet remaining Italian. The riches of the Italian populations could not be lost to the other nations and would be distributed within the larger Italy within Italy itself.

In the beginning, Italians were interested in the boundaries of their previous empire. They were seeking to demonstrate their desire to restore Mare Nostrum, or Our Sea which was the ancient Roman symbol of the Tyrrhenian Sea. The region became a powerful symbol under the Nazi regime. in World War II, the Italians had military control over the area at first time in the history of the time of the Roman Empire.

The notion of creating the idea of a new territory, or even a set of territory out of the peninsula, to take in Italian immigration and develop Italian nationalism was initially focused on areas with significant expatriate Italian communities already in existence. This is why Tunisia and, less so, Tripoli and the Egyptian city of Alexandria was the first and the most obvious regions that could be considered. Tunis was also the location of an important province of the Roman Province of Carthage which was a major part of Rome as well as the Italians believed the claim of an Italian protectorate of the area was an inevitable conclusion.

In the 1930s, Mussolini was making serious promises to secure the possibility of an Italian claim on Ethiopia. At that point, the time of colonial acquiescence was all but over and in reality, Britain as well as France had already begun to think about an era of post-imperialism. India began to begin negotiations for an end of its relationship with Britain and the rest of the major settled kingdoms have redefined their relations to Britain as the commonwealth. Ethiopia was then, under the leadership of the King Haile Selassie, was a participant in the League of Nations, so it was recognised as a sovereign republic which meant that Italy could require an extremely strong reason or an all-encompassing declaration of war in order to go forward with the military invasion.

Haile Selassie

While this was happening, under the façade in international mediatory and negotiations, Italy began massing troops in Eritrea. Italy in the meantime existed in the Allied camp in that the old agreements with Britain endured long enough to allow Mussolini to be integrated into French-Anglo-French alliances to fight German fascism. Both the French or the British could be willing to accept the Italian taking over of Ethiopia This eventually ended a consistent alignment of British and Italian interest. Mussolini declared himself to be a German all-weather partner as well, and so the formation of the Axis alliance was initiated.

The Italian invasion of Ethiopia was launched in the late year of 1935. The difference was that this time the attack would not be led by a colonial force of indigenous troops, but rather with a mechanized, modern army. Against this, the Ethiopians were not able to stand. In the end, almost without resistance, the Ethiopians fell. In 1936, the Emperor Haile Selassie fled the country.

Italian East Africa now included the territory that is now part of Eritrea, Somali and Ethiopia. The only areas in the region that weren't, at the time being Italian and included British Somaliland as well as French Somaliland The former was an attached territory located on the opposite side of the Red Sea from the vital British port of Aden as well as the later contemporary Djibouti. Furthermore, after France collapsed in June of 1940, and Vichy France was put into force and French Somaliland was declared, practically speaking an Axis region.

Furthermore, Italy held one more significant region within Africa which was Libya. It was the foundation of the Axis participation with North Africa as a theatre of World War II, and it served as the basis on the which Italian strength and adroitness in military, test against an actual adversary and a real adversary, showed itself to be much weaker than its components.

In Italy It was the Italian incident in Libya which was the turning point of Italian colonial adventures and established the stage for the brief, but troubled occupation of the land. Tripoli was considered to be the Italian second prize after the French were in control of Tunisia. Despite that, it fulfilled the standards of Italian respectability in the post-fascist era as well as being an important strategic area considering its position in the Italian military occupation over Ethiopia as well as Somalia.

Furthermore there was the fact that it was a testament to the Roman influence within North Africa was no less deeply rooted in the coasts of Libya as Tunisia, so that the old, unredentist tradition that Mussolini was seeking to create between his own regime and the splendor of early Rome could be accomplished by the Italian victory over Libya.

The very first Italian entrance into Libya was both mercantile and social in nature, so it was relatively innocuous. A kind of slow-moving policy which could, either by choice or chance establish the base of an Italian population in the area, Italian business (banking in particular) was able to enter the country in the midst of a gradual flow of Italian exiles. It is true that metropolitan areas including Tripoli were quickly sucked into this fashion however, no significant culture-related incursions to the vast interior of the country was likely under the circumstances. As time passed, however,

Italian capitalists and businessmen started to take control of the majority of Libyan commerce, banking communication, transportation and banking.

Mussolini in Ethiopia

In the meantime, Mussolini was trying to figure out ways to bring his military in action without the risk of triggering sanctions from big powers in the world, who would not let an invasion by an independent nation like Ethiopia was -a new politician was born within Europe in a bid that could rival the Mussolini's "star": Adolf Hitler.

The relationship between Mussolini and Hitler was not a happy one. The eventual dictator of Germany was a fan of the Duce and regarded the Italian Fascist instance to be an integral element of his rise to his position of power. Mussolini On his part, viewed Hitler's rise to power within Germany as a threat to the very existence of Germany. Hitler's desire to add Austria to

Germany did not align with the Italian defense policy, which had the immediate consequence of trading a tiny and vulnerable neighbor to one of the largest and most dangerous forces within Europe. Relations among Germany with Italy were fraught and no person, in that time could have anticipated to see the fateful alliance which was to join with the Fascist nations.

Methodical and patient work was unsuitable for Mussolini's style of thinking as was evident in the case of this incident this was highlighted when he attempted to come up with diplomatic strategies to ward off a violent response from France as well as England in the event of his attack on Ethiopia. As per Mussolini's plans to the letter, the Italian press painted a dazzling illustration for the people and declared the possibility that Italy might shut down its access to the Mediterranean Sea and attack Suez and Malta, which are both which were both under British control if required. After the declaration of war, the Fascist government argued that the war a defensive one by citing the border conflicts they created as casus belli. However, nobody believed them. In response, the League of Nations reacted swiftly by imposing severe economic sanctions against Italy and the rest of Europe, but this was not the last time they intervened.

In a sense on a military scale, fighting on the military level in Ethiopia was straightforward since the Italians faced an opponent who was completely superior in terms of the equipment, preparedness, and organization and also without planes or planes to speak of.

The Italians were to discover in the following decade that they weren't prepared to fight as they believed they were, and that Ethiopia did not have any agricultural resources, or even fertile soil to provide. In order to be economically profitable the country required an enormous level of effort and investments that Mussolini's Italy could not manage to afford. The tax burden to fund the war cost a lot of an already burdened population and economic sanctions hampered from the Italian economy. Through one decision, Mussolini diminished his power in the economy and his diplomatic status as he was struggling to find an all-weather ally. Hitler as well as his Germany would have been the anchor Italy required at the time as a condition of Mussolini's consent to annexe Austria. [23]

This could be deterring a different person from making rash choices in the future, however, Mussolini had a way of rationalizing the disastrous venture in order to prove that his sense of intuition was unshakeable. No one will ever determine if a calm, rational Mussolini could have helped make the Ethiopian victory work through making investments in the development of the area, as well as easing his brutal suppression of dissent as well as ensuring a steady peace in order to allow the Italian economic recovery.

After Ethiopia's victory, Ethiopia the president went right back to the preparations for war like no one had changed. He kept tensions in the repressive and economic sectors constant. This helped in for the development of an anti-Fascist group that was gradually gaining momentum underground, as the people were be no longer take on the regime's brutality towards the people. A lot of people who lived around the Duce claimed that he appeared to be in secret, much like was the case during his public speeches in public. He was always sporting the disguise as his "great dictator" like he began to accept his own propaganda. [25]

Chapter 9: The Path To Another War

The Nazis were in control of Germany by 1933. Since then, extreme right-wing parties as well as the left gained popularity across other countries which included Spain. It was clear that the Soviet Union was already the center of the authoritarian communist system and the rest of the democracies were fervently avoiding having to get involved in a new violent conflict. British and French officials were responding to the demands of their constituents by following policy of appeasement in the 1930s. So it ought to be no surprise that both sought to maintain their neutrality over Spain in the aftermath of the 1936 revolt. Britain was attempting to create the neutrality pact or non-intervention agreement to prevent the participation of the different European nations. While all parties seemed to be in agreement however, Germany under Hitler's Germany as well as Mussolini's

Italy rejected the agreement and already began with the provision of Nationalist troops with military gear in late 1936. France is, however is more keen than Britain to aid Republican Spain. French Premier Leon Blum was himself head of the left-leaning Popular Front coalition and saw close ties to his Spanish family members. The French population, however was much less enthused over involvement in Spain This resulted in Blum's notion of non-intervention. 29 September 1936 there was a "Non-Intervention Commission" was established in London with Britain, France, Germany, Italy and the USSR. Naturally, the rules were frequently and gravely violated and made a mockery of the stated purpose.

As the British and French determined to not be involved with Spain The support for the republic came through two major sources: International volunteers as well as those from the Soviet Union. (29, 30) The Soviets provided military advisers along with some soldiers and weapons to Spain Much of it required to be paid through the Republican government, who deposited their gold reserves. There was a downside of this dependence on the USSR to provide military aid was the increased authoritarianism of the Republican Army, and diktats coming from Moscow that was at the time ruled by the dictator Joseph Stalin. The Nationalists however, on their part, were able to receive assistance from the beginning of the war, from Italy as well as Germany. German Juncker planes were instrumental in transporting an Army of Africa across the Strait of Gibraltar in 1936 as well as its Condor Legion bombed Republican zones and most notably in Guernica within Guernica, in Basque Country.

An image of Soviet personnel and cars in Spain

Mussolini's Italy was a more extensive source of support. Italy had backed fascist and conservative political parties prior to the conflict and later provided 60,000 soldiers and weapons when the war was first triggered. Italian forces were vital in numerous conflicts, with the most notable being the capture from Malaga within Andalusia. Though their support to the Republican party was substantial but the help offered to Nationalists proved to be more efficient in consistency, consistency, as well as on a larger scale.

This resulted in balance of power was heavily tilted to Franco's favor. Republicans were determined to keep the their hopes alive till the conclusion of the war that democratic powers would be able to intervene to prevent a total loss. This was to end up being a foolish hope.

The Battle of the Ebro was the longest-running and biggest battle during the Spanish Civil War, lasting between July and November 1938. The battle took place under the dark of night on July 24th, Republican troops were able to cross across the Ebro and cut off some of the Nationalist communications lines. Initial groups formed by that Republican army then moved 25 km to Ganesa. The morale of Republicans increased as the Nationalist forces became anxious thinking that the resolution of the battle was in sight. [33]

Like other key conflicts during the Civil War, but the initial Republican gains were defeated by Nationalists which then crushed their adversaries to death in the final battle, before retaking the territory they lost. From August to October, the region surrounding the Ebro River was the site of bloody and desperate clashes. [34It was clear that the Republicans knew that the survival of their country was dependent on the outcome of this fight. However, in the end, the Republicans began to be weakened slowly by the ferocious assault of Nationalists and their total dominance on the air. In November 16 the Nationalists had forced the Republicans over their initial position which meant that the Battle of the Ebro was concluded. Both sides, particularly the Republicans have suffered massive loss, with estimates of 10,000 and 50,000 deaths.

The situation was becoming clearer that the Republicans did not have a chance to achieve success in conflict, and the leaders looked for ways to get out of the war, or a way to bring an end to the war. The worst part was that the bulk of the Republican management was now based situated in Barcelona and in the locality of Catalonia where they appeared to be becoming and isolated. The Republic has a huge area of land in between Madrid and Valencia to the central and south of the country. However, it became a matter of when, not whether, Franco achieved his final victory.

As there was a Battle of the Ebro was in full swing at the time of September 1938, European powers met in Munich. Munich Conference, which turned into among the more notorious events in the twentieth century. It also paved the path to World War II by abandoning Czechoslovakia to the Nazis and establishing the notion that "appeasement" as a geopolitical ploy in the years to come, Munich also had implications regarding and influenced the Spanish Civil War.

It was the Munich Agreement was eventually signed by Hitler, Mussolini, British Premier Neville Chamberlain, and French president Edouard Daladier. Supposedly, it was a way to stop Hitler from invading the "Sudetenland" region in Czechoslovakia with its large number of ethnic Germans The democratic authorities accepted Hitler's demands in Munich as a condition for an assurance of a larger peaceful world and a guarantee that Germany will not take over any additional territories. The result, however turned out to be a disaster. When Munich was over and he was able to get what was wanted, Hitler began a wave of British-based anti-British propaganda. This included the personal insults he hurled at Chamberlain. The Fuhrer was so bold as to say that an accord with a democratically elected government should be considered to be temporary when Churchill or Eden was replaced by Chamberlain the German leader was expecting war and had his strategies to prepare for war with this scenario in his mind. He also was planning to push west with no British provocations after he had completed his work in the east.

The leaders from Munich

Following Munich was over, the Wehrmacht were able to swarm across the border to the Sudetenland and the Czech troops grudgingly retreated from its mountain positions and fortifications. The troops of 34 divisions disengaged from an imposing defense line, without firing a shot. 175,000 common citizens fled trying to stay away from German command. The Czechs had no illusions about Hitler's persona or the nature of Nazi Germany's social and cultural system and 50,000 others soon following the first panicked evacuation.

The territorial gains of Germany in Czechoslovakia were more than just a slice of real estate. The areas that had large populations of ethnic Germans included

Czechoslovakia's mountain ranges that border the country and the massive fortifications. The Munich Agreement stripped away the exterior of the country and revealed its defenseless interior regions. The whole process was akin to the result of opening up a bank vault's gates for a burglar and hoping that the robber would not take the cash inside. Unsurprisingly, the Nazis took the initiative further than that the Munich Agreement permitted, though they did not take control of Czechoslovakia completely. The Gestapo were sweeping into the country in the form of black slugs, seized more than 10,000 suspected or known to be anti-Nazi and put them in Concentration camps. The decree of Hitler dismissed 50,000 Czechs from the Sudetenland out of work and handed them over to Germans rather than the Nazis also banned the Czech languages in the areas they had control over.

Extending the provisions that were stipulated in and enforcing the terms of Munich Agreement from the start in 1938, The Third Reich carved off two vast areas of territory that were given to Poland and the other to Hungary. The Kristallnacht violent attack on Jews between November 9 and 10 and 9-10, 1938 was extended to the recently acquired Sudeten territory, which affirmed the policy of hatred that Hitler enacted as an official characteristic for ethnic Germans within and beyond the borders of Germany. All the while, Chamberlain responded to this protest in the typical way. "'Oh how boring are these Germans are!' declared Neville Chamberlain when he read the news reports about Jewish riots in Germany as well as the punishments that followed. "Just as we began to see some advancement!" (Leibovitz 1997, 1666).

The accord reached in Munich has also impacted also in Spain. It also showed Franco that Britain as well as France did not have the stomach for conflict and thus appeared likely to not intervene in Spain in any way. Similar to the previous point, Munich also affected the Republican strategy because, in the absence for French or British support in the event of a crisis, the Republic was at in the hands of Franco as well as the fascist power. Munich was also a proof that democracies were misguided in they had not taken note of the Spanish rebels. Refusing to intervene and turning a blind and oblivious to Italy and Germany's intervention, Britain and France had maintained the policy of appeasement to Spain. This encouraged Hitler as well as Mussolini as well, but now the these events became more serious. Even with Chamberlain's "peace within our time" statements of Chamberlain the world was beginning to become shockingly obvious to many Europeans that a war was on the horizon in Europe during the 1930s and would be a bigger threat than even the Spanish Civil War.

When Hitler tried to test France as well as Great Britain's patience with the expansion of regions, Mussolini was leading his own war to explore the limits of peace. He engaged within the boundaries of his own nations. In a series of speeches addressed for the people the dictator declared Italy as the dominant Mediterranean power, and cited Corsica, Nizza, and Tunisia as potential targets to include in the Italian space, which was contrary to those who took advantage of every opportunity to display their love for peace. One of the most obvious instances that this distinction between the war-mongering government as well as the population that was more peace-oriented highlighted was during the Neville Chamberlain's trip to Rome in 1939. It was the British premier's final effort to stop conflict. Chamberlain received a warm reception from crowds of cheering people eager to express their gratitude however, he was confronted with the wall when he began his behind talks behind closed doors with Mussolini and nothing was able to stop the Duce from taking part in the next major European war. [35]

As Hitler began his war towards Czechoslovakia, Mussolini took action to attack Albania which was a mistake because the country was within the Italian politically oriented orbit. The people who would be responsible for this assault in the army elite were aware of the plan just a few weeks prior to the start of the operation, which proved the rashness of it. Mussolini did not act on his emotions in order to prevent becoming a shadow of Hitler.

Like in Ethiopia however, the troops were assigned to battle an adversary that had virtually no ability to resistance. The occupation ended on April 19, 1939. The 22nd May, 1939 Mussolini offered the "Pact of Steel" that was a treaty between Germany with Italy. It was a pact which was difficult to break out of and was both offensive as well as defensive. The ruse and deceit were the mainstays of the relationships between Mussolini and Hitler mostly due to Mussolini's need to prove to his allies the fact that Italy could be a formidable and stable country that was capable of taking on an upcoming war.

It's very likely that Mussolini was deceived by the military elite because he continually urged for more regiments to be raised and to strengthen their forces with more equipment and numbers. In the absence of resources, the generals were left with no choice but to form an "paper army." It was comprised of unfinished units, and stretching the capabilities of beyond what Italy was able to field within an ever-growing military, it looked amazing on the paper list that was given to the Duce however, in reality the army was not able to last a single campaign. Ironically, the military was so essential to the Mussolini's power ideology political power, was one area that the Duce was completely beyond his capabilities. His war vision was a blend of what did he experience in his time in the First World War and romantic beliefs about how the soldiers battled with courage greater than the weapons or theories, and with even a thought of logistics and operational challenges. There would be no negative consequences had he allowed his commanders to perform their work, but just as with Hitler, Mussolini was adamant in his reign of war, constantly slapping heads with his army when it was still in a period of preparations in 1939.

The immediate result of this resulted in the dismissal of highest-ranking, most skilled military officials who were prepared to defy Duce's plans. The Italian Army was awash with"yes men" and "mediocre" officers whose main abilities were to maintain an extremely high standard of discipline within the ranks through the extensive recourse to physical discipline. For context: Mussolini offered Hitler 150 divisions and 10,000 soldiers on reserve. However, only 10 divisions with a fully operating value. The rest of the army were either insufficiently staffed or poorly equipped.

Ahead of the Start of World War II Sources in the vicinity of the Duce inform us that towards the end of 1939 after war became unavoidable, Mussolini was taken by doubts, frequently stating that keeping away from war while awaiting the impending British win was the most effective decision for Italy. But he also admitted that no one could let his war of a lifetime go unnoticed as well as he could not permit anyone to view the man as a coward. It was planned to take over and conquer Greece as well as Yugoslavia however, ultimately, the uncertainty and indecisiveness was buried in the event that Great Britain guaranteed Poland's independence at the time Hitler promised Mussolini his promise that British kept them off from the conflict.

In the end, the Duce discovered a way to keep from entering the battlefield with an army not prepared by stating that Italy was ready to join the war but would require 17,000 train trains of materials related to war. The number of trains was exaggerated enough that it was unacceptable, and Hitler's decision permitted Italy to stay "non-belligerent." The initial tactic, which was almost a betrayal, severely damaged the relationship between the two dictators.

Mussolini again chose to follow the option of least resistance in not joining the war at once However, he wasn't thrilled over this. You can feel his anger through the words he used in his speeches. In them, his speeches avoided terms like neutrality and promoted an "non-belligerent" term. In a fear of the possibility that Allies were likely to quickly overtake Germany He was keen to disown his allies and be a part of the side that won in the event that his fears became a realisation.

The cautious approach of Mussolini's to entering the war only lasted a few days. Germany attacked to the east, north and west, sweeping Poland, Denmark, and Norway off. German troops were already located in Belgium and were on an "unstoppable marches" which would split the British-French front in two by the time Mussolini ultimately made the decision to declare war fearful of missing his opportunity to be participant in the probably certain German victory.

After they had entered the conflict, Mussolini agreed with Hitler in a plan of war that they had formulated together which stated that the Italians were to invade North Africa and Greece, in addition to a modest offensive that would be launched against the almost defeated France. Mussolini was in favor of an "parallel war" where the Italians would be the main beneficiaries of fighting within Southern Europe to become the leading Mediterranean power. He also refused a proposal of tanks that were modern from Hitler in the month of June 1940. It was a weapon that could have been used by the Italian Army might have benefited from.

Prior to the conflict and the rising of fascism Italy resulted in French fear of invasions by the Italians and, as a result, France constructed smaller fortified areas that were facing to the Italian frontier. The French also constructed fortresses in the island of Corsica where Napoleon Bonaparte was born. Napoleon Bonaparte, in preparation for a seaborne attack of the Italians.

In the end, the most effective Maginot-style French defenses of 1940 were not on the frontiers of northeastern France to Germany rather in the southwest in Mussolini's Italy. The Italian dictator wanted a piece of France as well, and it sent armies of his to conquer his Gallic neighbours in protest to the advances of Hitler. Mussolini's desire for money and territorial agglomeration, more than any specific strategic need led to the planning of an Italian invasion of the south of France. Self-styled "Duce" was worried about the possibility that Hitler along with the Third Reich would seize all of French territories, including its manufacturing, monetary and agricultural wealth which would leave him with the lower value of his African empire. "On the 26th of May Mussolini took two of his top military subordinates: Marshal Pietro Badoglio [...] and Air Marshal Italo Balbo [...] in the hall of Palazzo Venezia in Rome. "If Italy was to take a seat on the Peace Conference table when the world's resources are to be distributed and she wants to be a part of the war quickly,' he declared. Balbo was tactful and inquired of Mussolini whether he was aware of exactly what he was doing. (Mitcham, 2008, 340).

Mussolini

From the perspective of Mussolini and his encroachment towards France could have seemed like a definite outcome. The Italians had 32 divisions to support their offensive westward, while the French operating their own "Little Maginot Line in the Alps" comprised just four divisions. The Italians had a huge advantage numerically. was a sign of a number of weaknesses in their favor and also certainly one advantage in favor of French soldiers. French Army. Italian soldiers during World War II exhibited lower in terms of quality in comparison to their German counterparts when it came to the training and equipment they had, as well as the most important aspect, their management. Italian armored vehicles in World War II displayed less impressive characteristics than those of virtually every other nation, with the exception of the Japanese and Italian tanks in particular, were equipped with an armor that was so thin that tiny guns often had trouble piercing the surface, and their guns were unable to penetrate the defenses of French lighter tanks not to mention medium tanks belonging to those of the British or Americans after the conflict.

Another obstacle that hindered the Italians' odds of achievement was in the land itself. In the Little Maginot Line of the Alps utilized advanced techniques for fortification used to defend the Northeastern forts, but had the benefit of powerful natural defenses offered by the mountains themselves. The British observer recognized and appreciated the advantages of these locations just a few years prior to Mussolini's envah. "Montgomery-Massingberd, who visited France in 1935, commented on the strength of the fortifications facing Italy - 'tunnelled as they are under 40 or 50 feet of rock, with embrasures for guns and machine guns covering every approach.'" (Black, 2012, 241-242).

Incredibly durable, and built using the same care and precision similar to the fortress line in northeastern Europe and the Little Maginot Line of the Alps had a restricted number of routes. The passes were only three or four that could support large troop movements while the less popular passes had a small number of passes for the French to keep an eye on.

Massive mountain ranges that were rugged dominated the scenery, Italians were forced to attack along a variety of appropriate routes, each that the French quickly recognized and protected. The numerical advantage of Mussolini's 32 divisions against 4 was not a actual military advantages with these restrictions on his troops and a meticulous, well-planned defensive planning of the French.

The most continuous segment began at the city of Menton in the Mediterranean coastline and continued northward along the Franco-Italian border over a distance of 33 miles. Forts were made up of infantry block - containing machines matched with embrasures for rifles or artillery blocks, making use of 75mm howitzers as well as 95mm cannon, which were never used in the Alpine areas.

The French put a lot of ouvrages into the region, with 22 large ouvrages as well as 22 smaller works. Because of the lessened threat from artillery on the terrain that was rugged, the French employed slightly less, thicker 9-foot cement roofs and walls. Drawbridges made of ponderous steel were often used to close the main entry point to the structure.

Fascist Italy initially considered the possibility of a partnership together with France against Germany early in the

1930s, but British pressure forced the French to beg Italian victories over Africa which pushed Mussolini into the camp of Hitler. So, Mussolini declared the war against France as well as Britain on the 10th of June in 1940. Mussolini did not inform Hitler of his plans as well as, for his part the Fuhrer declared open hostility to the Duce as well as his army as he instructed the Wehrmacht top commander (OKW) to deny requests for help or assistance from Italians.

As Germans coming into France specifically during June 13th through the 17th Mussolini's hope of capturing some of the ailing nation fell rapidly as his army rolled slowly into positions to strike. The Duce had his soldiers attack on the 18th of June however, even that late date proved to be unattainable. The 19th of June, when there were none of the Italian troops yet in French territory, Germans met with the newly-formed French regime that was headed by Marshal Petain about an armistice.

Mussolini determined to gain entry into the front door, forced his superiors to make it even more difficult for them to make the crossing into France in great displeasure. "Badoglio and Ciano opposed this move in the same way as striking an individual who was in a slump as well, and it certainly was a way to earn an Fascist dictator the ire from the majority of people around the globe. [...] It was the French confronted him by deploying General Rene Olry's Army of the Alps, [...] to the delight and delight of a lot, including most from the German General Staff, Olry fought the 32 Italian divisions for five days, and inflicted massive losses on the Italians." (Mitcham 2009, 345).

Chapter 10: Italy And Benito Mussolini

Even though Italy was one of the victory-winning forces during World War I, but Italy towards the start of the 20th century there was an erupting of anger. Social problems that were long unsolved like the plight of rural areas, the effects of late industrialization, the displacement of veteran soldiers and the resentment between clergy and leftists triggered conflict and uncertainty about the viability of the system of parliamentary politics as a is a good governance model.

The left-wing radicals wanted to tackle problems as radical similar to those of socialist Russia and to scare the middle class, which is more and more susceptible to the enticement of the extreme right and their call to take a firm stand against the risks of Bolshevism. A large portion of Italians to restore the national stability and establishing its supreme power status skilledly employed former socialist politician and journalist Benito Mussolini. He was the leader of fascist revolution, and in the month of October 1922, he forced the monarch to choose him as the position of prime minister.

The magazine Historical of the 24th of November was dedicated to the persona of Benito Mussolini, the personality who is now a sort of model of current right-wing dictators. In the years prior to the 85th year, the fascist militiamen's march to Rome which, at the close of which was Benito Mussolini at the head of the government. While Italy continued to be a monarchy during the first years of the Mussolini time period, they were at most, they were formally democratic. Actually, the entire authority was exercised for over two decades was held by the Leader and his closest collaborators. What is the way this can occur in a nation with the long-standing tradition of liberalism, humanism and Renaissance? Similar questions were posed to the moderator for guests of Petra Broda's historians Ondrej Houska (OH) of the editor of Czech Radio 6 and Pavel Helan (PH) of The Hussite Theological Faculty of Charles University in Prague as well as from The University of Pisa.

PH: He was raised in an isolated area close to Forli. His mother taught as was his father, blacksmith. His father was the co-founder of his own party, the Italian Socialist Party, so it is no surprise that Mussolini was born from a evident radical leftist culture. In the end, up to 30th birthday the politician remained and continued to work. He left in the start of the 20th century Switzerland (both due to the fact that, in the interest of avoiding military service and also to get a job) the medallion of Karl Marx in his pocket. Although he was not the most rigid

Marxist (i took a little from Pareto who's lectures I heard were heard in Switzerland was listened to) unique and positioned was appointed director of the principal sheet socialist Avanti an extreme faction that was part of the Italian Socialists.

If it splits into the Italian Socialist Party? What are the reasons behind the breakup?

The OH: For Mussolini as well as others of his generation it was among the primary motives that led to the to the outbreak of the First World War. Italian Socialist Party had complied with a pacifist policy, and theoretically was to follow the policies of all European socialists, but this was not the case. In the beginning, 1914 was when Mussolini the course he took with his political parties was in agreement. However, over time but, in the end, we do not agree with him in the sense that it was in line with nationalist passions as well as nationalism. Actually, Italy into World War was a part of his entry in 1914 but was neutral. It was an enormous and tense debate over whether or not to join the war. Mussolini during this conflict ended up arguing on the side of intervention. This implies a split with his Italian Socialist Party.

Ph: I'm not certain whether in 1914, it was from Mussolini having clearly embraced nationalism. Nationalist concepts are starting to be understood in the First World War, but in the end, it was his heart, concerned about the opposition. They still feel socialist, and believe that the Revolution was initiated by the war, and is worried that, the victory in Germany and then imposes an Prussian government that is reactionary throughout Europe. In the period 1914-15, his motives are not nationalist. This happens after the conclusion in the First World War.

As it's the final day of First World War, nationalist has a tendency to oppose international socialist policies?

PH: Yes. Sometime in 1918 he wrote (and opposes its previous texts) that socialism does not have to be uniquely protinacionalisticky. It is at this time it is still regarded as socialist.

What is the cause of the current crisis? Benito Mussolini in early 20s was elected to the presidency?

The OH: Italy was a victorious power during World War I, but it was the midst of not being stagnant and was in an extremely difficult position. In particular, the political landscape in Italy was extremely divided. The reason fascism came to power due to the fact that the elements of the Italian political scene that were determined to protect the current regime didn't have the mass-popular party of commonsense; Italian liberalism was strongly party-oriented. However, both socialists and fascists but the clergy also had this massive base. Following the introduction of an electoral system that was based on proportional voting which these parties have overwhelmingly were able to record.

In addition the the former Italian Premier Giovanni Giolitti included fascists in the coalition he formed, and it has been made by the salonfahig (satisfactory). The whole thing is in sync. It is not yet mentioned some of the factors like poverty factory storms, rural areas and factories. Due to what we could discuss over for a lengthy time.

What was the fascist ideology that was proclaimed? What is its distinction from other extreme currents? What is the role that it played in the conflict?

PH: Violence played an important role. Perhaps Nolte has the most exact definition. He states that fascism is a response to Bolshevism in the same way and that violence. That is the premise. This ideology is, despite the emergence of the fascist revolution in 1919 differs from fascism in the thirty years earlier. It is in fact different from Nazism cannot provide an explanation of the constant concepts of fascism. However, the ideology actually changes. In the early days of fascism, it was an the anticlerical Republican. The Fascist programme of 1919 is an extremely left-wing program as well as the right-wing plan, but it is based on the eight-hour work time and securing funds to those returning from suffering as war widows. This is clearly a social requirement.

Chapter 11: What Sort Of Environment Mussolini Lived In?

A great role was played by the masses of troops returning from the war. The focus was on the small bourgeoisie. People belonging to this category get beaten on the streets since the officers are considered to be being the perpetrators of guerre. They put themselves in danger they were away, only to return to his home country, and their public credit has dwindled, and are and are not considered to be a part of society. A lot of people seek different experiences but some of them are unable to be accepted back into normal society. The elements mentioned above can't simply be able to capture Mussolini. Most often, they fight to be the socialist cause. A reaction from the Socialists to violence followed by a swift and violent reaction from the fascist side. These movements were often able to recruit members as well as Socialists

However, they only recruited those who didn't want to change their ways. Bolshevik the Bolshevik way.

In the 20 years that followed Mussolini He repressed all other social and political organizations, trade unions as well as political parties. We can conclude that Italy was a 1930s a totalitarian regime?

Oh: Fascism himself so he was aware of. The term "totalitarian" was in no circumstance not been considered a derogatory term. However they were aiming to build a totalitarian government. For instance, in the Italian situation, however, there is no way to speak of an absolute state. Theoretically, it is true that Mussolini asserted that Italy is a nation of totalitarians However, for everyday life of the those living in rural areas as well as in urban areas and cities, fascism was a major factor. Religious, familial and relationships between patrons and clients within the lives of Italians were the norm. In the remote areas of Italy there are those who had never had a clue about Mussolini.

Do you feel that this was a stumbling block to the essence of the Italian national identity and it was not a good chance to become a lasting system of governance?

There was a problem it was that, at the time it was difficult to talk about it. It was that they would be one nation of Italians. The idea was that everyone Italians are indeed Italy. Family and regional identity were important to them, but they were also. There were also objective motives for the fact that fascism was not able to form an all-encompassing group of Italians that would be preparing for conflict.

The word "violence" is used here. The Fascist system can comprehended in terms of military repression and the preparation for conflict. However, it was more cliche and not so in actual practice.

Shortly after assuming power Mussolini started to implement an expansionist foreign policy. What were his first actions? Which of them actually lead to these steps?

HP: He had tried in 1923, by occupying by the Greek island Corfu and was unsuccessful. If these developments continue. The culmination was Abyssinia around the middle of the 30s. This was the initial step taken in ensuring that there was an association between with fascist Italy to Nazi Germany. Often it was an expression of a statement. The verbalizations were associated with a specific theatre and opera. Furthermore, Mussolini's policies were only until the time of union with Germany during the late 30s that also had some issues constant. It is somewhat a bit influenced by the "Sacro individualism" of Italian policies during in the First World War.

That's the truth of his ideas? Mussolini was a man of principle or was he simply an opportunity seeker that was never without strength?

The PH: I can't believe that there was ever. Perhaps it was because it was that he split from his Italian Socialist Party, it was among the few Neoportunistickych decisions. Other than that, it was purely the consequences of opportunism. He also admired German fascism. But believed that Hitler could be victorious in the war so he spoken to the German leader. He first met her as a child, she thought that he was crazy. That's why Mussolini could clearly claim that the man was an opportunist, and that the majority of his choices were based upon opportunity.

Oh: I don't agree slightly with the idea that Mussolini was a consistent plan for expansion. In the majority of Italian historiography, however, some historians claim that, in the late 20s the plan was geared to the spread of fascism. The idea of establishing an Mediterranean empire was fundamental to understanding fascism. It would certainly be at odds with France as well as Britain. Personally, I believe that this was the real basis of Mussolini's policies.

He was not able to undertake an expansive step, as the conditions of 20s to 30s were not allowing him. He was forced to change. The evidence earlier in the 20s was a probe into the German extreme right's strategies for forming a new alliance with France. After the mid-30s, that radically altered the global political landscape, Mussolini would allow his program to be followed.

It has attacked Abyssinia and is which is now Ethiopia in which his troops was bankrupt over the end?

OH: It's not. The battle against Abyssinia in response to logistical needs and what it represented for Italian soldiers, was success. The result was not a triumphant victory without difficulties However, it was an extremely successful war. It is possible that Edvard Benes believed that everyone Italians could do it, they would only through great difficulty and could result in the fall of fascism. It was a waste of time and only came into existence following Italy took on Abyssinia in the sense that Abyssinia was an untapped black hole that sucked the money that was derived from practically nothing. Italy didn't have.

The PH says that economically, there is nothing. However, on the political front, Mussolini triumphs by a huge majority. When the war is over, sanctions against

Italy are essentially suffering. Mussolini is regarded as someone who can stand in the face of the entire world. This is the greatest victory he has ever had. It's the biggest triumph for Italians as a result of, Arturo Labriola, who was a staunch opponent of Mussolini's government along with many others, had a strong stance been a part of the scene when Mussolini took on Abyssinia in the 1930s. Add what makes France together with England critiques us when we just would like their country to be theirs as they already have one. There's even a type of peak where the entire nation is united and Mussolini enjoys his supporters.

OH: The notion is linked to Italy and the Italians in Abyssinia which resulted in a sort of war between colonial powers. This was not the typical colonial war that ended in France as well as Britain. Mussolini saw it as an entirely different kind of warfare, a total war. In the instructions for the war include things such as that Italy is granted Abyssinia Abyssinian in the absence of these. It wasn't an imperial mission and the war was conducted with complete deployment of the available Italian militaries.

Italian goals for war were evident in The Second World War, in which Italy was a participant in the war until 1940?

In the words of PH, Italy at the time of 1940 wasn't prepared, and is the main reason why it was not ready. Italian soldiers. This was due to it was because Mussolini was looking forward to take a seat at the table of winners. The main reason was. The decision he made to join World War II went against major parts of the Italians and even an overwhelming portion of fascists, who opposed an collaboration that was formed with Nazi Germany.

The military's setbacks North Africa, Greece, and elsewhere. can eventually bring about its demise in 1943. They thought that the fascists were able to keep the Mussolini regime intact but what if?

OH It's a difficult to answer. These are the evidence that the 30th reign of the king, pope as well as some top-ranking Italian fascists like Farinachi Robero as well as Dino Grandi private confessed that God knows what is going to take place following Mussolini. According to the laws that were in force then, the next leader would need to be a king who will choose a successor upon the death of his predecessor. This is a controversial issue, it is difficult to make any assumptions.

The PH Mussolini as the father of his chosen his successor, Galeazzo Ciano. He was the foreign minister. However, his death was in the 30s. This leaves the question unanswered.

After the joining of Benito Mussolini in 1943, the Germans were able to hold it over just two years while remaining in the free world. The time was spent in the northern part of Italy which was where he also established an Italian republic that had its capital at Salo. This, however, was a symphony during the time it was his puppet at the control of Germans. After being slain by Italian militants, his remains later embarked on a journey which ended at his home. What was his connection to Central Europe?

Ph: Very interesting. As a child, Mussolini published a work on John Hus that has for many years been the only book on Hus in Italian that was named Jan Hus, a man who was a man of the truth. The book also translated pages which Huss was able to write in Constance and he also translating Luther's preface.

Mussolini in Huss as seen as a the figure of Huss as a model for a certain type of movements that are able to defend its true beliefs. Mussolini was at the time an excellent anticlerical and so it is possible to consider as an example man named Hus, who was burned to death in the Catholic Church because of its truth. The reason was the fact that he was in contact with the group Free Thought, which was in preparation for 1915's Congress in Prague and she was planning to extend the role of Husa to other countries.

Chapter 12: There Mussolini Was Seeking Help

The dividing line from Central European and Italian fascist regimes and fighting extremism in Central European countries Was Mussolini a supporter of the fascists and similar to those in Central Europe? Was there the support of Italian Central

European countries, as well as the democratic opposition?

Oh: Mussolini previously stated that fascism was not an exportable commodity however the truth was quite different. Perhaps in Austria was the Nazi-inspired Heimwehr movement, which Italy as well as Hungary is heavily backed by weapons and money but only to be thrown out by the Austrian Social Democrats. Austrian democracy restored in an administration that was more fit Italy. Czechoslovakia also supported Austrian Social Democrats, so it is possible that Italy and Czechoslovakia that directly crossed paths. There are also documents showing that, in 1924, the Italian anti-fascist party received funds from Czechoslovakia and its provider was direct T. G. Masaryk. This conflict between democracy and fascism has more than just ideological origins and is founded on differing political views of how to organize within Central Europe.

How can we enjoy a successful fascist movements with a large basis in places like Poland, Hungary, Czechoslovakia?

Did you experience PH? Was it an alternative situation. Italian Fascism was a particular case. It was a particular form of fascism in Hungary, Austria and, naturally, within our own movement. They want to be like them, but just a small portion. Furthermore there are the Czech fascists rarely appear in the similar to the Italian fascists, simply because they're often in the slovanofilove. They are, in this case, bound to their policies are in contrast to Mussolini.

It is known that they are under certain influences of fascist ideology within contemporary Italy. Is this influence strong enough?

The OH is a minor influence. It is, however, not among the circles of Italy thought of as a negative, unambiguous phenomenon. In the present, the National Alliance, a major Italian right-wing political party is called the post-fascist. Despite this it is widely acknowledged the fact that its leader Gianfranco Fini is truly a democratic. But, the National Alliance has deep fascist roots. The party is on it's Italian right, however, there are some truly fascist groups (well-known Alessandra Mussolini) however, there are also a few extremist components.

The terrible events of Nazism as well as during the Second World War overshadowed in the minds of generations postwar of Italian fascism's contribution to the rise of violent trends throughout the world in the early second half of the century. It is possible that this contributed to the fact that the end of fascism has also been a blessing by a lot of Italians. They did not come to an end following the 1945 pillories similarly to a defeated Germany but soon back to the democratic community of Western democratic democracies.

People who only know those who only know from Mussolini film footage that he was an expert comical grimaces and velikasskych gestures can easily overlook the fact that for millions of Europeans as well as Africans were the Italian Duce comical figure however, he was the vile enemy who left bloody tracks throughout their lives. War machine and fascist repression specifically reached the extreme perfectionism that was the hallmark of the Nazi's Third Reich, but this shouldn't be the reason to disregard the threat that he posed to Western civilisation.

The execution took place at his feet in a gasoline station. His death was a frightening thought for Hitler

The only way to be certain about the causes of the demise of Italian dictator Benito Mussolini is that at the bottom of the corpses suspended from the construction site bombed petrol station in Milan.

Photographs preserved show the head of the dictator who was executed as well as the marks of a number of punches. The image isn't pretty but, as we all know the possibility of ending British prime minister Winston Churchill profoundly disgusted. The same was impressed with another policy towards the close of their lives, German Chancellor Adolf Hitler. He was believed to be in the wake of news accounts of the execution Benito Mussolini decided to end his own life and allow it to his body burn. The body of the man was displayed as a trophy in Red Square as happened with the body of Benito Mussolini in Milan.

It is important to note that by the end of April 1945 sixty-two year aged Benito Mussolini just a shadow of the person he was in his twenties and thirty-somethings. This could was the case at a minimum to be the case in the beginning of conflict. When he left Italy fortunes during war, the dictator, though diminished. The office workers in his company heard the groans of pain. Mussolini had gastric ulcers by lying across the ground. In a state of sleep, and then during the summer of 1943, when his most trusted companions in the Party was deposed, he seemed to feel any relief. In any case, he can't refuse to even stay in an Abruzzo mountain hotel. hills of Abruzzo.

The man stayed in the area until September, at which point the group was kidnapped by a German group. Mussolini became the puppet of Hitler, in the role of head of the "Republic of Salo" located in Northern Italy. Under the aegis of and the supervision of the SS Cold technocrats, they have implemented the reign of terror like Italy is not yet experiencing. The SS began the expulsion of Jews to camps for extermination, secret police instituted hunts for those who remained with the shadow of fear. From 1943 until the year 1945 Mussolini changed into a person who was not a universally disregarded. In addition, he was able to take anger over the demotion of his demise, his son was also counted Galeazzo Ciano. As a family-oriented Italians the emotional pain was as well.

The conclusion of World War II Benito Mussolini is on the loose. At the Swiss frontier, the convoy together with his entourage disintegrated as spring snow.

Then, they leave with his the mistress Clara Petacciova, driver and assistant, as well as a small group consisting of German soldiers. Mussolini dressed as a basic German soldier as his path crossed 52. Partisan Brigade "Luigi Clerici" (guerrilla executed in 1944 by Nazis at the time of 1944). His face was so well-known that he helped even with a German soldier in his uniform. Duce was uncovered as a partisan, upon hearing the name Bill and was detained immediately. It is possible that Mussolinoho traded in the commander of the German columns to guarantee peace and safe travel towards Switzerland. There is a possibility, however the evidence isn't there.

How does death

Walter Audisio, antifascist fighter and communist, also known as Colonel Valerio on the 28th of April 1945 Mussolini entered the bedroom of the farm located in Bonzaniga. The man claimed he was seeking to overthrow the dictator, and also his love interest's assistance to get out. It's hard to tell if it did or not. Mussolini or not, it just was forced to accept. Together, they drove the car towards Belmonte. Villa Belmonte. The Petacciovou also was shot after they left the vehicle. were killed.

The official Italian as well as the more likely scenario. The end of powerful men never ceases to stir the imagination which has led to the creation of numerous stories and speculations (since the original version was rewritten and at best, proven). Another version states that Walter Audisio April 28 in the same building that they held Mussolini and Petacciova as well as announcing that the Committee of National Liberation him was sentenced to execution. They were later taken to an unmarked alleyway in which five rebels were executed.

Based on other theories, Mussolini didn't shoot rebels, but rather individuals from the British intelligence agency after they took evidence-based documents which Mussolini carried along with her gold. Another version of the story claims that Mussolini as well as Petacciova did not get shot, however, they died because of the brutality of by guerrillas. According to some reports, they died naked as their clothing was found to contain in bloody traces and following the execution, there was no one allowed to conduct an autopsy (in actual fact, an autopsy took place).

There are varying reports on the behavior and the actions of Mussolini during the final moments. Maybe he quit, or perhaps up until the very last moment of his upset. Last words might be written upon the monument once it had been removed.

The fate that followed the bodies of Benito Mussolini and his mistress is well-known. They first traveled to Azzone on 29 April 1945. They were also together with the other fascist leaders, they were hanging upside-down from the beams that were bombed at the Esso petrol station at Piazza Loreto, Milan in Italy, which is at the time that they were executed by the Germans killed the guerrillas on August 10, 1944. The death was shameful as well as the humiliation for all of all fascism. The mass grave of the man she was in love with for 20 years, was tortured and mocked. Then, when it was done they were interred in the cemetery of the town. The coffin that contained those of Benito Mussolini in 1957 he relocated to his home town of Predappio in Italy, where it was buried in his family's burial ground.

www.ingramcontent.com/pod-product-compliance
Lightning Source LLC
Chambersburg PA
CBHW071439080526
44587CB00014B/1920